CRAFTS STUDY CENTRE

Essays for the Opening

Edited by Simon Olding and Pat Carter

Canterton Books

CRAFTS STUDY CENTRE

Essays for the Opening

Edited by Simon Olding and Pat Carter

ISBN 0-9541627-4-9

Published by Canterton Books
Forest Ford
Brook
Hampshire SO43 7HH
U.K.

www.cantertonbooks.co.uk

Distributed by the Crafts Study Centre, University College
The Surrey Institute of Art & Design
Falkner Road
Farnham
Surrey GU9 7DS

Book design by Sarah Jackson

First published June 2004

Contents

FOREWORD

Sir Christopher Frayling
Chairman, Crafts Study Centre 1982 - 2004

2

In his autobiography *Double Harness*, the etcher and teacher Robin Tanner recalled: 'A group of friends – craftsmen and educationists – met from time to time in the late 1960s, to discuss the possibility of founding not a museum of objects untouchable behind glass but a living, expanding Study Centre where work could be held in the hand and enjoyed, and a whole archive consulted'.

These craftspeople and educationists – including Henry Hammond, Muriel Rose, Marianne Straub and of course Robin Tanner – were united in their vision of practitioners, teachers, scholars, disciples and the interested public being able to benefit from the work and example of the pioneers of modern craft through a living collection augmented by records, writings and papers. Too many galleries, they thought, simply exploited people's growing interest in the subject. The point was to enhance it. Later, this vision would be described by the critic Peter Dormer as 'a British Museum, if you will, of the crafts'.

The founders were united, too, in their admiration for the pioneer inter-war generation of British craftspeople – the generation roughly between William Morris and the rise of art school crafts: Bernard Leach, Katharine Pleydell-Bouverie and Michael Cardew (potters); Rita Beales, Ethel Mairet, Phyllis Barron and Dorothy Larcher (textile weavers and printers); Ernest Gimson and the Barnsleys (craftsmen in wood); Edward Johnston, Graily Hewitt and Irene Wellington (calligraphers). Looking back - and it may seem a strange thing to write - they were in some ways the equivalent among craftspeople of the Modernist generation in the fine arts. The heart of the Study Centre would be the work of these pioneers, plus that of the founders; the guiding principle, at a time of increasing mechanization and de-skilling, would be 'that the processes of purpose, planning and making are one'.

And so, as Robin Tanner added: 'painfully, slowly, and with characteristically English altruism and amateurishness, the idea of a collection of the best work of the twentieth century... was born'. By June 1977, ten years after those discussions began in Euston Road, the original Crafts Study Centre had opened in Bath 'on a beautiful evening when the cuckoo was still calling, loud and long'.

'The first block print designed by Dorothy Larcher', Old Flower, from volume one of the record of Barron and Larcher's block-printed textiles, c 1923.

© Crafts Study Centre

4

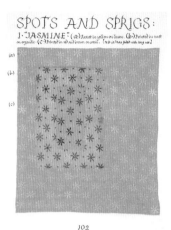

The reference to the cuckoo wasn't just fanciful - it also referred to the fact that a lot of people along the way had thought the idea of the Centre belonged in cloud-cuckoo-land. 'Sometimes', said Tanner, 'we came near to despair'. But thanks to the generosity of the pioneers, the founders and of Robin and Heather Tanner (who donated the royalties of their books *Wiltshire Village* and *Woodland Plants,* among others), the beautiful evening finally arrived. Since then, under the careful and committed curatorship of Barley Roscoe and Simon Olding, the Crafts Study Centre has grown into a world-class resource for the study of twentieth century and contemporary British crafts. Its collection is unrivalled, its writings and papers a fascinating archive for practitioners and scholars alike.

One of the challenges in the meantime has been relating the work of the pioneers to more recent currents of practice. I became Chairman of the Trustees of the Centre in the early 1980s, and can remember many

'Spots and sprigs' from volume one of the Barron and Larcher record compiled by Robin Tanner

© Crafts Study Centre

lively discussions with fellow Trustees and members of Acquisitions Committees about the crafts today. How did the Leach tradition of form and function relate to today's pots where form follows fiction? How did the textiles of Barron and Larcher speak to today's students of printed textiles? Would it be possible to reconstruct Muriel Rose's gallery layout, and would it still work? Should embroidery be in or out? Did anyone remember the elephants at the British Empire exhibition in Wembley, 1924? No? Or the Oxshott Pottery's elephants which were exhibited in 1967? Oh, *those* elephants. It was very important to build bridges between the core collection and subsequent work which was in sympathy with it, so that the Centre would indeed be 'living and expanding'. The discussions wandered sometimes, but we always arrived there in the end.

At last, in summer 2004, thirty-seven years after the initial discussions, twenty-seven years after the original Centre opened, twenty-two years after I chaired my first meeting - with Robin Tanner, Henry Hammond and Marianne Straub still in good voice - the Crafts Study Centre has its own freestanding gallery, close to the teaching and research of The Surrey Institute of Art & Design which has done so much to enable the building to happen. The idea that 'work could be held in the hand' may have proved a little ambitious by today's curatorial standards, but in all other respects the dreams of the founders have at last come true. As the great linen weaver Rita Beales wrote to the Tanners about that beautiful evening when the cuckoo was still calling: 'I am still in a kind of dream… It is a great achievement and I know it will grow and grow and grow - what an asset for the Craft world'.

Photograph of Robin Tanner
In 1981 by Dennis Thorpe
© The Guardian/Dennis Thorpe

HISTORY

Barley Roscoe

A history of the Crafts Study Centre
collections and archive

'Painfully, slowly and with characteristically English altruism and amateurishness, the idea of a collection of the best work of the 20th century artist-craftsman was born - not just a museum collection, but one that, augmented by craftsmen's records, writings, and papers, could be handled and seriously studied and enjoyed'.[1]

This is how Robin Tanner, the etcher, educationist and founder Trustee of the Crafts Study Centre described its tentative beginnings in a '1st Birthday' lecture on 1 June 1978 which he gave in Bath at the Holburne Museum of Art where the Crafts Study Centre had opened the year before. In 1977 the official opening had actually had to extend over three days so that all the numerous people involved from its inception could be invited. The weaver Rita Beales spoke for many in a letter of thanks she wrote shortly afterwards:

I am still in a kind of dream, picturing or trying to picture all the "sweat and toil" and love that you have put into the creating of our Crafts Study Centre. How grateful craftsmen should feel, both the old and young ones to come along later on. It is a great achievement and I know it will grow and grow and grow - what an asset for the Craft world.[2]

In fact the first spark of the idea for the Crafts Study Centre goes right back to 1964 and the death of the hand-blockprinter, Phyllis Barron, on 23 November. In her will she left all her life's work together with that of her partner, Dorothy Larcher, to the etcher and educationist Robin Tanner with the words 'I leave all my work to Robin. He will know what to do with it'.[3] She was absolutely right - he did. Between 1965-7 Robin and his wife, Heather, mounted three memorial exhibitions in annual succession. The first was in Painswick, Gloucestershire where Barron and Larcher had lived since 1930; followed by a larger exhibition at the Royal West of England Academy, Bristol, and subsequently another at Cheltenham Art Gallery and Museum.

The display of these women's remarkable collection of hand-blockprinted textiles together with associated material prompted many people to urge that a permanent home should be found for their work. This was no easy matter. The Crafts Advisory Committee (subsequently to become the Crafts Council) had not yet been founded and there was

Barron and Larcher, length of blue cotton with a discharge block print 'French lines' 1923-40

© Crafts Study Centre

only a handful of museums that showed even a mild interest in British crafts post 1930, let alone contemporary work. A determined group, many of them friends of Robin and Heather Tanner and those who had known Phyllis Barron and Dorothy Larcher well, held their first meeting in London to explore possibilities on 11 November 1967. At the meeting Muriel Rose, a doyenne of twentieth century crafts and later to become a founding Trustee of the Crafts Study Centre:

> reminded those present of the origin of the meeting. The exhibitions of the Barron and Larcher textiles had shown the urgency not only of keeping such work together, but also of securing work of similar quality by other craftsmen (themselves possibly exercised as to where to bequeath it) while it was still available. Together each collection would enhance the other, both visually and educationally. Where might such a collection be housed?[4]

In order to answer this burning question and find a permanent home for the collections, the group recognised that it was essential to clarify ideas into a document that could be widely circulated. A statement of policy and aims was drafted and clearly shows on what lines the concept of a Study Centre for the crafts was developing:

> There is in Great Britain no permanent comprehensive collection of the work of outstanding artist-craftsmen of our own century. A group of concerned people, craftsmen and educationists, propose to bring together the best of this in order to conserve it and to make it freely available for enjoyment and study.
>
> The present moment offers unique opportunities to assemble, before it is irretrievably dispersed, examples of the output of those pioneers, such as Bernard Leach, who began work after the First World War, and who found themselves obliged to rediscover, largely by trial and error, many of the techniques which industrial development had obscured or retarded. Their work shows not only a finely judged sense of quality in their choice of material but also a deep understanding of basic simplicities, giving it today a particular value for education at all levels from the young child to the adult. It establishes a criterion of craftsmanship and could be a continuing source of inspiration not only

for the ordinary visitor but for student and professional, through whom could come a strong influence upon industrial design. A body of work of this quality, in pottery, wood, metal, woven and printed textiles, embroidery, is already available as, for example, the substantial collection of block-printed textiles left by Phyllis Barron and Dorothy Larcher and, if it could be properly housed, more would be readily contributed or bequeathed.

It is therefore proposed to raise funds to establish a centre, which must necessarily be attached to an existing institution such as a university or museum, with easy access. To maintain continued liveliness, changing exhibitions, including work from overseas, are also envisaged. There would be library space not only for books but for personal records, notebooks and other manuscripts, and room where reserve collections could be handled at leisure, giving exceptional opportunities for first-hand study.[5]

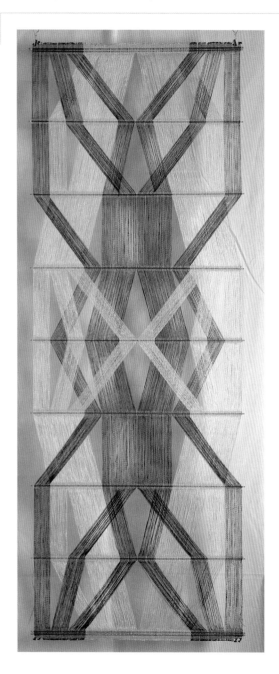

Peter Collingwood, Metal plaque
M.81 No 5 Macrogauze, 1981

© Peter Collingwood/
Crafts Study Centre, 2004

Numerous venues where the collections might be housed were mooted and over the coming months locations explored in Guildford, West Dean and Farnham as well as Bristol and Bath. Meanwhile progress continued, slow but sure, in formalising the status of the group and on 1 April 1970 the Crafts Study Centre attained charitable status with Ewart Uncles, a potter and educationist, taking the Chair. At the same time the collection was growing apace thanks to promises on all sides, as Robin Tanner recalled in his autobiography:

> Our friend Bernard Leach said he would readily lodge a collection of his pots with us if we could find a home. Katharine Pleydell-Bouverie offered the same. Rita Beales - surely the greatest of linen weavers - announced that I was one of her executors, and that the fine collection of her incomparable hand-spun, vegetable-dyed, hand-woven linens was ours as soon as we could house it. Other friends were ready to give calligraphy by Edward Johnston, Graily Hewitt, and Irene Wellington, furniture by Gimson and the Barnsleys, and the residue of weaving done by Ethel Mairet and those associated with her.[6]

Of the various locations being pursued as a possible home for the Crafts Study Centre (CSC) the Trustees favoured The Holburne of Menstrie Museum (now The Holburne Museum of Art), a Georgian building standing in its own grounds at the top of Great Pulteney Street, five minutes from the centre of Bath. First built as the Sydney Hotel it had been acquired by the Trustees of the Holburne in 1913 and converted by Sir Reginald Blomfield to house the fine and decorative art collections of Sir Thomas William Holburne (1793-1874). Links between the Museum and the University of Bath had been forged in the late 1960s. The Holburne Trustees together with the University welcomed the idea of embracing the CSC. At a dinner held on 23 October 1970, the Vice-Chancellor of the University of Bath was able to give the assurance that 'Senate offered a definite invitation to the Crafts Study Centre, since not only was the University keen to have it but co-operation from representatives of the Holburne and the City Council was evident'.[7]

An outline proposal was put forward to build an extension at the back of the museum which was to include accommodation for the CSC. Needless to say the Crafts Study Centre, as the bride, was expected to

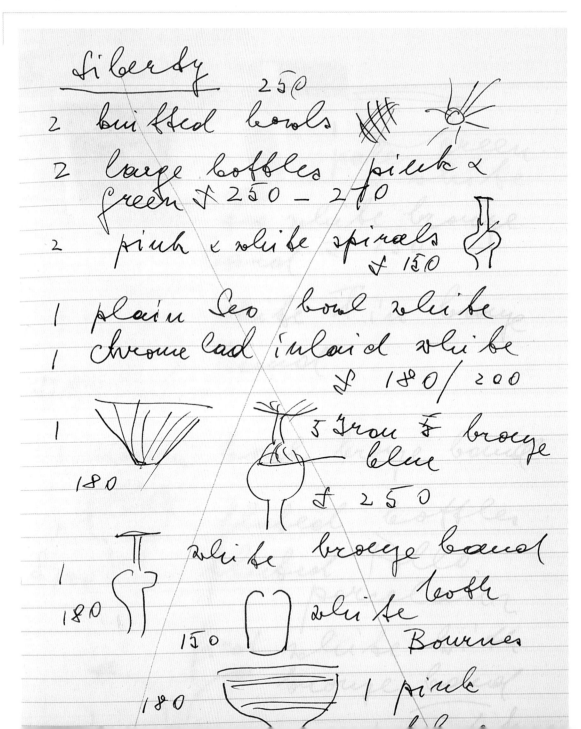

Liberty   250

2 knitted bowls

2 large bottles pink &
   green ✕ 250 - 270

2 pink & white spirals
                    ✕ 150

1 plain Leo bowl white
1 chrome lad inlaid white
                    ✕ 180/ 200

1   5 Iron & bronze
                         blue
   180   ✕ 250

1   white bronze band
                         both
   180   white
         150   Bournes

   180   1 pink

bring at least a modest dowry rather than move in penniless; fund-raising had to begin in earnest. However, as Robin Tanner recalled 'the struggle to raise funds to establish a Centre was long and frustrating'.[8] It was to be another seven years before the partnership was fully forged and the CSC could at last open its doors to the public within the Holburne Museum. Amongst the Trustees:

> The Tanners were stalwart fund-raisers, both giving generously themselves and attracting donations and support. Robin gave a talk to the Friends of the Museum which reassured and enthused and it was agreed that an exhibition of the proposed Crafts Study Centre collection should be mounted at the Holburne during July and August 1972. With able assistance… Robin master-minded the mounting of the exhibition and organised publication of the catalogue, which provided a lasting record and served as an excellent aid in encouraging donations.[9]

The following year Ewart Uncles retired and James Noel White, formerly with the Council of Industrial Design and a leading figure in the World Crafts Council, was appointed Chairman of the Crafts Study Centre. In 1981 he was to be succeeded by Robert Goodden, former Pro-Rector of the Royal College of Art and Chairman of the Crafts Council, followed in 1982 for over 20 years by Christopher Frayling, who was to become Rector of the Royal College of Art and in 2004 Chairman of Arts Council England. James Noel White recognised the urgent need of drawing up a preliminary list and catalogue of all the work promised to the Centre when it opened and a grant was secured from the Ernest Cook Trust to appoint a part-time research assistant to visit prospective donors and catalogue the work that had been proffered.

At the same time it was becoming increasingly apparent that the large grants needed for major building work were not going to be forthcoming and reluctantly, in 1975, it was decided to abandon the plans for an extension to the Holburne. Instead, half of the ground floor of the Museum was offered to the Crafts Study Centre. This space had formerly been the resident caretaker's flat but with his retirement and the installation of a new security system, it was now vacant and available. Although this was a much more modest start than originally

Lucie Rie archive, order book, c 1980-83

©.Yvonne Meyer/ Crafts Study Centre, 2004

had been envisaged, the Crafts Study Centre Trustees decided to accept the offer rather than delay an opening any further. The following year, a generous grant from the Crafts Council enabled this space to be skilfully converted by Neville Ward Associates to form an L-shaped permanent exhibition area, separate study room-cum-office and store. High ceilings, neutral colours and light, natural wood fittings created a spacious and uncluttered effect and served to show work from the permanent craft collections to advantage. In 1994, further space on the first floor of the Holburne Museum was converted on similar lines by Fielden and Clegg to provide an archive study room and library in memory of Robin and Heather Tanner. Small temporary exhibitions were sometimes mounted within the CSC's permanent galleries, whilst those on a larger scale could be shown in the more extensive temporary exhibition galleries of the Holburne Museum which were shared with the Centre. From the part-time post of Research Assistant for the Crafts Study Centre, Barley Roscoe was appointed full-time to run it, and later, was to become the Director of the Holburne Museum and Crafts Study Centre.

Here over more than two decades, the CSC obtained an international reputation as a unique collection and archive of British crafts from 1900 onwards. Strongest in work of the first half of the twentieth century, more contemporary exhibits were added through gift and purchase on the recommendation of the Acquisitions Committee comprised of leading figures in each area represented in the CSC collections. Major figures in the craft world played a significant role in the growth of the collection and archive through donation and bequest, their generosity often encouraging further gifts. To the profound gratitude of all the Trustees and with particular encouragement from both Muriel Rose together with Henry Hammond, the potter and educationist, Bernard Leach offered to present nearly 100 of his pots to the Centre together with his source collection, and subsequently bequeathed his archive. In addition Katharine Pleydell-Bouverie, one of Leach's first students at St Ives, gave a substantial collection of her pots to the CSC together with fine examples of work by her friends and contemporaries Michael Cardew and Norah Braden. As former Head of Ceramics at the West Surrey College of Art & Design, Farnham (subsequently The Surrey Institute of Art & Design, University College), Henry Hammond went on to bequeath his archive to the Centre together with pieces from his

collection. Latterly the CSC was very fortunate to receive the coveted Lucie Rie archive which complemented an impressive group of work in the collection by Lucie Rie and Hans Coper, two of the most significant figures in British post-war pottery.

Turning to textiles, the collection of two of the most talented British hand-blockprinters of the 1920s-30s, Phyllis Barron and Dorothy Larcher, which Robin Tanner had been bequeathed and which had inspired the founding of the CSC, included lengths, garments, samples, printing blocks and source material. Subsequently Susan Bosence, who had felt compelled to start blockprinting textiles on first seeing their work in the late 1940s, placed her own collection and archive with the Centre. Marianne Straub, a weaver and founder Trustee of the CSC who had been the executor for Ethel Mairet, herself an important and influential figure in the weaving world from the 1920s onwards, ensured that Ethel Mairet's Workshop was fully represented.

It was also one of the first collections in the CSC to be the subject of substantial research culminating in a publication and exhibition. Having benefited from a grant from the Worshipful Company of Weavers and support from the Crafts Council, Margot Coatts was appointed to work on this material which led to the publication of *A Weaver's Life: Ethel Mairet 1872-1952* (the first in a series of joint publications with the Crafts Council), and a touring exhibition which was shown in Bath, Birmingham and London [during 1983-4].[10]

Ella McLeod, Head of Textiles at the West Surrey College of Art & Design placed a representative and significant group of weaving by Elizabeth Peacock with the collection, whilst Rita Beales not only donated and bequeathed her collection of finely woven linen and wool textiles but also munificently bequeathed her entire estate to the Centre.

The calligraphy collection of the CSC, which developed from the choice collection of the calligraphy expert and Trustee, Heather Child, was to become the most substantial body of 20th century British calligraphy outside London, much used by teachers and students of lettering as well as scholars, as an indispensable source of reference and research. Work by two of the most important figures in the history of modern calligraphy, Edward Johnston and Irene Wellington, was placed in the Centre thanks to the generosity of the Johnston family and Irene Wellington herself, whilst grants from Leverhulme and the Crafts Council facilitated their research and documentation. A full catalogue of the Edward Johnston collection was made by Justin Howes and published in 1987, while Heather Collins catalogued the Irene Wellington collection and went on to contribute to the publication *More Than Fine Writing* together with Heather Child, Ann Hechle and Donald Jackson (Pelham Books, 1986;

Elizabeth Peacock, one of three cottage tapestries, hand woven in 5 narrow strips, 1960-69

© Amelia Uden/
Crafts Study Centre, 2004

British Library, 1998). The first publication coincided with a major retrospective of Irene Wellington's work initiated by the Crafts Study Centre, and helped make the CSC one of the foremost beneficiaries for donations and bequests of 20th century calligraphy and lettering.

> The long loan of nearly 100 exhibits from the Crafts Council collection for over a decade made an excellent complement to work in the CSC and enabled the museum to show a full range of work spanning the century. Many of these pieces played an important part in redisplaying work from the Holburne Museum and Crafts Study Centre where exhibits were placed in stimulating juxtaposition to provoke comparisons and contrasts of colour, form, scale, texture and content as well as date, material and technique. This prompted the inclusion of the Holburne Museum and Crafts Study Centre as a case study in *Contemporary Crafts in Museums* published by Southern Arts (1996). In addition the Crafts Study Centre's collection was well used for research by students, craftspeople and the general public on a day to day basis. Study facilities, available by appointment on weekdays, were frequently used by students and groups from colleges, schools, specialist societies and practising craftspeople. Degree students studied various areas of the collection as part of their course work, while art tutors often found it useful to bring classes to the Centre to draw and handle work.[11]

From the beginning requests for loans from the permanent collections were made for exhibitions of national and international importance. Over the last decade ceramics have been lent for major retrospectives of Lucie Rie and Hans Coper at the Barbican, London, and again to The Museum of Applied Arts, Vienna. Key pieces from Bernard Leach's collection and archive toured Japan in *Bernard Leach, Potter and Artist* with a final showing at the Crafts Council, London in 1998. Emmanuel Cooper's biography *Bernard Leach, Life and Work* was published by Yale University Press in 2003, the author fully acknowledging how much his research had depended on access to the Leach archive in the Centre. The publication of the book coincided with the end of the tour of an exhibition *Bernard Leach: Concept & Form* at the National Museum and Gallery of Wales, Cardiff to which the Centre had made a substantial loan of pots and drawings. In the same way, a large body of woven material

Ethel Mairet, woven tartan length, late 1940s

from Ethel Mairet's Workshop was lent for a major touring exhibition in Japan entitled *The English Arts and Crafts Movement and Shoji Hamada.* Loans of Barron and Larcher's work together with other printed textiles from the collection were lent for various exhibitions including *Colour into Cloth* mounted as a touring exhibition by the Crafts Council in association with the Centre, *Modern Britain 1929-1939* at the Design Museum, London and the touring exhibition *Pleasures of Peace*, initiated by the Sainsbury Centre for Visual Arts.

From its inception the CSC maintained an energetic exhibition and events programme including lectures, demonstrations, seminars and study days. As already shown, many of these were initiated by the Centre and drew on the permanent collection, with illustrated catalogues and related publications providing a lasting record. In addition major touring exhibitions that had originated elsewhere were hosted by the CSC such as, latterly, *Codes and Messages: Lettering Today* (Crafts Council) and *Peter Collingwood - Master Weaver* (firstsite, Colchester).

The move of the CSC to The Surrey Institute of Art & Design, University College in spring 2000 developed from a recommendation made during work conducted for the Holburne Museum and Crafts Study Centre by Bonnar Keenlyside Consultants following on from a preliminary study by Simon Olding and Crispin Paine:

> Thanks to a grant from the Arts Council of England in 1997 Bonnar Keenlyside originally were appointed to explore the feasibility of building a purpose built extension to the Holburne Museum to accommodate the CSC and provide improved joint facilities. However, having concluded that this was not a viable option Bonnar Keenlyside went on to recommend that the CSC should seek another partner. The two bodies of Trustees recognised that this would be in the interests of both parties as not only would this release much needed space within the existing building for further displays of the Holburne's collections, but also allow the Study Centre to expand and develop its potential to the full. Possibilities for consideration were listed, while editorials in *Crafts* magazine and the *Museums Journal* stimulated a good response. A short list was drawn up, offers invited and exploratory visits made. The field was narrowed and, after much discussion and deliberation including further follow up visits, Trustees agreed that a partnership with the Institute would be in the very best interests of the CSC for the long term future.
>
> Historically, many of the founder members of the Study Centre [such as Henry Hammond, Ella McLeod and Susan Bosence] had close links with the Institute, and this partnership [now] looked to support both organisations' core aims in fostering excellence in the teaching, research and development of modern crafts, whilst also facilitating wider public and academic access of an invaluable resource.[12]

The Institute was firmly committed to building dedicated space for the Centre on campus, and in the interim it was agreed the collections would be accommodated in accessible storage nearby in Farnham. Digitisation of the collection, together with a significant proportion of textual items

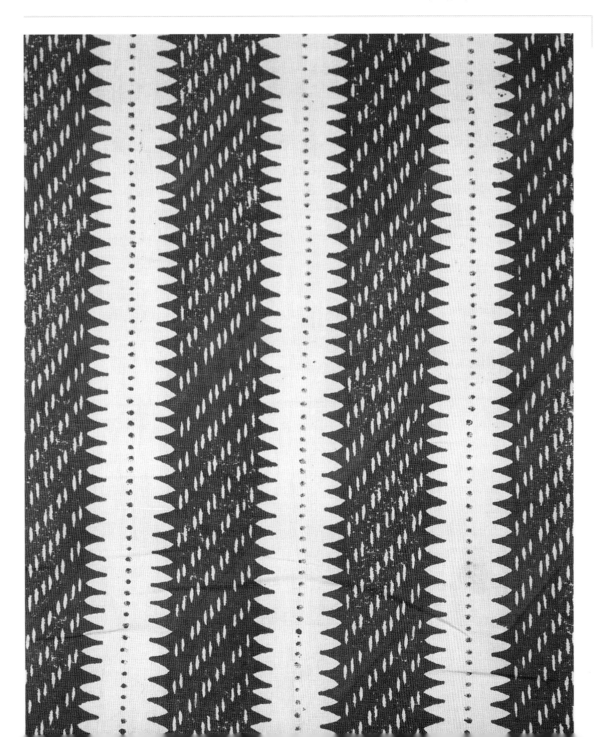

from part of the archive, was seen as key to managing the documentation of its collections and archive efficiently, whilst enabling the CSC to raise its profile by making itself accessible worldwide. The CSC swiftly benefited from its new partnership with the Institute for, in May 2000 and within a month of the collections moving to Farnham, an award of £194,000 was made to the Institute through the Joint Information Systems Committee (JISC) of the British Higher Education Funding Councils. This funding, together with an additional grant from the Headley Trust, meant the CSC was now in a position to proceed with its planned digitisation project. The outcome of this project would be the production of digital resource material, featuring some 3,000 images from the collection and 1,000 documents from the archive, together with a selection of associated teaching and learning materials. It was most encouraging to have such immediate positive evidence of the mutual benefits of the partnership between the CSC and the Institute from its inception and together be able to look forward to a bright future ahead.

'The History of the Crafts Study Centre' has drawn closely on 'Robin Tanner and the Crafts Study Centre' by Barley Roscoe, published in *Tributes to Robin Tanner 1904-1988* (Crafts Study Centre, 1990) and 'New Horizons for the Crafts Study Centre and Archive', a paper presented by Barley Roscoe to the OECD/IMHE seminar on University Museums, Paris, September 2000 (Organisation for Economic Co-operation and Development, 2001), both of which provide further detail than space allows in this essay.

[1] Robin Tanner, 'Phyllis Barron (1890-1964) and Dorothy Larcher (1884-1952) as I knew them', unpublished lecture given at the Holburne Museum and Crafts Study Centre, Bath, 1 June 1978. Quoted by Barley Roscoe, 'Robin Tanner and the Crafts Study Centre' in *Tributes to Robin Tanner 1904-1988* (Crafts Study Centre, 1990)

[2] Barley Roscoe, 'Robin Tanner and the Crafts Study Centre' in *Tributes to Robin Tanner 1904-1988* (Crafts Study Centre, 1990)

[3] Robin Tanner, *Double Harness* (Impact Books, London, 1987) p168

[4] Minutes of the first meeting to discuss the proposed permanent collection of the work of Twentieth Century Artist Craftsmen, held at Friends House, London, NW1, 11 November 1967

[5] Crafts collection statement of Policy and Aims, 1 October 1968

[6] See 3, p179

[7] Minutes of the meeting of the Crafts Study Centre Trustees, held at 2 Manchester Square, London W1, 21 November 1970

[8] See 3, p180

[9] See 2, p17. The exhibition *20th Century Craftsmanship* was held at the Holburne Museum from 10 July – 5 August 1972.

[10] Barley Roscoe, 'New Horizons for the Crafts Study Centre and Archive', paper presented at OECD/IMHE Seminar on University Museums, Paris, September 2000. Published in *Managing University Museums* (Organisation for Economic Co-operation and Development, 2001)

[11] Ibid

[12] Ibid

CERAMICS

Edmund de Waal
Ceramics: the need for a new history

28

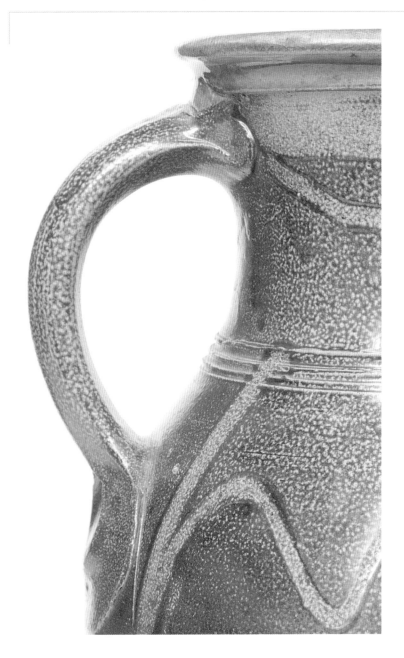

Michael Casson, jug, salt glazed
stoneware, 1983

© Michael Casson/
Crafts Study Centre, 2004

I

In an age of transients, of artists who use any material that comes to hand, material is a conceptual matrix of some complexity. As Nicholas Penny pointed out, materials carry with them both explicit and implicit values. These are to do with their intrinsic worth, their scarcity or abundance, the difficulty or ease of their working, their resemblances and metaphoric possibilities. The adoption of a material to use in making a work of art is never neutral: not only does it immediately inflect the values just mentioned but it also reflects the values of the artist. To use your own blood, as Marc Quinn has done with *Self*, is to comment on raw material in a visceral way. But whether an artist chooses to be a catholic in their choice of materials or not is an issue: for some critics there remains the slightly distasteful feeling that to adopt a single material is somewhat fetishistic, slightly 'crafty'. There is a historic weight to this. The engagement - sometimes bordering on obsession - with locality and specific raw materials is immediately bound up with ideas of authenticity within the world of the British crafts. This can lead to the sense of an elect, who have been allowed access to the Truth of Materials. There is the question of definition: are you a ceramic sculptor or a sculptor, a bookbinder or an artist? The material and the discipline haunt the critical language. A sculptor like Richard Deacon engages with new materials and processes with a sense of empirical enquiry: will this idea be more interesting manifest in perspex, bent wood, clay or blown glass? But that this should be so does not invalidate the value of adopting a particular material to work in. An absorption, even a passionate absorption in a material does not, *a priori,* stop you thinking. It isn't the end of a journey. Material is not a final safety blanket.

The problem of how to critique or to contextualise work made with clay has emerged again and again. This is partly because clay can be messy, inchoate, primal, sensual. It seems to invite anxiety about status. It is so lowly in the pantheon of materials that some critics and curators seem challenged that artists used the materials at all. Its image is also beset by the cliché of 'The Potter's Wheel', the interlude between television programmes or the stopgap when something went wrong. That seductive image of a formless lump of clay, a great wet and inert mass being coaxed into control with confident speed, a shape emerging from

30

chaos, of hands and clay working together. It remains the basic, grounding, Ur image of the potter at work. The resonances are manifold: Adam was created from the clay, clay artefacts are amongst the earliest known works made by humans. Fired clay - malleable earth made hard through its interaction with fire - is all around us; geologically, historically, architecturally. It is part of our culture, part of our metaphorical language, one of the ways that we define ourselves.

Given this, and looking back at a century of ceramics, the super abundance of things made from clay and, in the main, fired, it may seem obtuse to comment on how fragile the definitions of ceramics still seem. There is a plethora of self-definitions: 'potter', 'ceramicist', 'ceramist', 'maker', 'artist-in-clay'. There have also been visitors to the worlds of ceramics: painters, sculptors, designers, industrial manufacturers and architects who can all justifiably claim attention as having been involved in defining what ceramics mean. In the last century ceramics have been used for avant-garde polemic, for nationalist rhetoric or for cultural retrenchment. Ceramic work has been exhibited alongside wildly different media, and in so many bizarre ways and places. Ceramics have been made to impress, for solace, to educate, to reflect the propriety of the maker or the painter, for personal or for national self-aggrandisement. There have been attempts at criticism by potters themselves, by art critics, poets and writers, as well as dealers and curators. New ways of talking about the changing disciplines of ceramics and studio pottery emerged. Some histories have been written, much has yet to be written. What has been little discussed is the fluidity between these worlds and allegiances: the craft potters who also design for industry, Picasso's influence on sculptural ceramics, the ways in which a political climate has helped to create a particular emphasis on 'appropriate' and 'inappropriate' forms. While there are cabalistic redoubts, where particular entrenched positions are still held, where a technique or a canon of pots are still considered to be normative, it is more difficult than ever to keep out the flux of images and ideas that swirl around.

Anxieties have led to an endless reiteration of questions about where objects made from clay belong, of how pots made by potters sit alongside ceramic work made by sculptors, artists, architects. This is part of the rather weary narrative around clay. These questions over status

clear galena
& thin slip

cream

milk

1045

can obscure - and frequently do - the central question of what is worth taking seriously in ceramics today.

It is a contemporary question. The galleries are full of clay. Grayson Perry has won the Turner Prize. Antony Gormley's *Field* in its many international, trans-cultural, manifestations fills central spaces in museums and the liminal spaces of deserted industry. Tate St Ives has initiated a series of collaborations and installations that have seen spaces taken over by Kei Ito, Martin Smith and Richard Slee. Rebecca Warren's unfired clay sculptures with their accretions of classical reference and of pop imagery are omnipresent. They are part of a complex art world: the most expensive ceramic artefact sold at auction is not a piece of Sung imperial pottery but Jeff Koons's porcelain model of Michael Jackson with Bubbles, his pet monkey. This tells us a little about aesthetics and a lot about not understanding the complexity of the art worlds.

So what is going on? There are some curious reversals of engagement. It is no longer unusual to find potters forsaking the plinth and table top to make work that occupies more complex spaces. Though the domestic pot - the studio pot - remains important, ceramics now are much more than a domestic drama. They have a public, and interrogative, face. The intersection between architecture, ceramics and sculptural installation has become a key site of exploration. They are also overtly politicised as in Perry's decorative, tabloid pillaging of ceramic history. Perry uses the idioms of the classical vase (as made in an evening class) onto which he paints scenes of suburban despair: a welter of graffiti, consumerism and sex.

The cry of 'the barriers are down' rings through every generation: barriers are always down and are always being resurrected. Ceramics have been part of the different worlds of craft, design, architecture and art throughout the last century. Pots have played their part in most of the leading art movements, but what happens next?

With the increasing speed of internationalism, it is now no longer possible to guess where a piece of work was made. All the indicators of specific regionality (I belong here, my work is part of this vernacular tradition) are flattened out into a common style. At its most basic level, what were once highly culturally mediated techniques are now commonplace. There are now more 'anagama' type Japanese style wood firing kilns in America than in Japan, 'raku' is omnipresent and English slipware turns up in the work of Korean students. This level of quotation, technical, stylistic is part of the fragmentation of post-modernity. It is more a question of how you are perceived to quote than whether you do or not.

In the art world that has become 'dematerialised' - where the art work is often an absence or a fleeting record of a presence through video or performance, actual objects made in actual places have a particular resonance. There will be a continued interest in performance with clay - often using clay's inherent ability to move through different states from liquid slip to malleable material to fragility. But pots will continue to state their meaning strongly in the world.

II

It is not rare to find a vocal discipline - music, for instance, is crammed with talented commentators. Within the crafts, pottery does stand out for its noisiness. Making pots and writing about pots are deeply entwined activities in the history of post-war studio pottery in Britain. Only Lucie Rie seems to have kept silent. Everyone else seems to have written. There is a plethora of books, articles, manifestos, travelogues, critiques, autobiography, poetry and histories as well as the constant stream of letters and reviews that filled *Pottery Quarterly* and *Ceramic Review*, the new magazines dedicated to the discipline. Much of the writing was technical in name, but shot through with strongly value-driven discussions of where the place of techniques lay. Such books as Michael Cardew's *Pioneer Pottery* and Michael Casson's *The Art of the Potter* helped to redefine the landscape of how to make pots. Other potters like Alan Caiger-Smith managed to resurrect a whole tradition - in his case that of lustres - through painstaking scholarly research.

From Bernard Leach and Michael Cardew of the pioneer studio-pottery generation, to the young turks of the 1960s like Tony Birks and Michael Casson, and the contemporary critical commentaries of Alison Britton, Emmanuel Cooper and Julian Stair, there have been sustained attempts to articulate a vision for pottery. The mood has ranged from the elegiac to the furious. Very occasionally, as with Hans Coper's only extant piece of writing, it has even been beautiful:

> A pre-dynastic Egyptian pot, roughly egg-shaped, the size of my hand: made thousands of years ago, possibly by a slave, it has survived in more than one sense. A humble, passive, somehow absurd object - yet potent, mysterious, sensuous. It conveys no comment, no self-expression, but it seems to contain and reflect its maker and the human world it inhabits, to contribute its minute quantum of energy - and homage.

But, even with this remarkable act of self-definition, ceramic history is still in its infancy. The study of the studio pottery movement, the idea of a Crafts Study Centre at all, is still radical. How to map this discipline is problematic. Is it a late grandchild of Ruskinian Art Pottery - the

Bernard Leach, stoneware bottle, 1969

© David Leach/ Crafts Study Centre, 2004

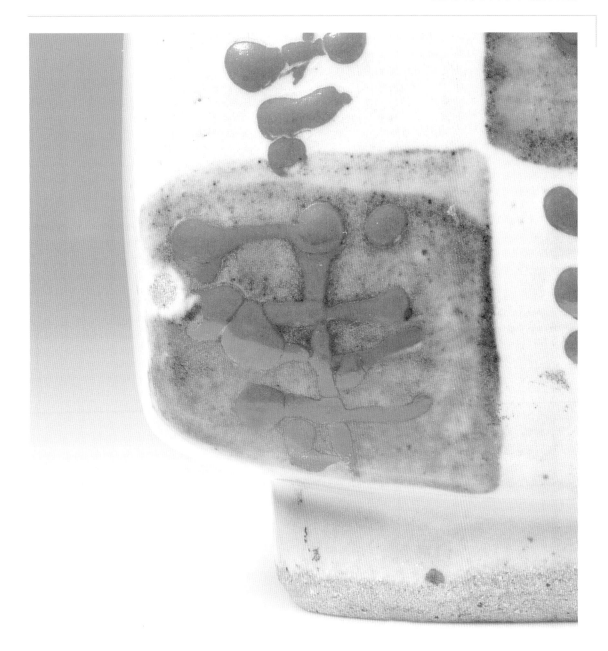

continuation of William de Morgan or the Martin Brothers? Is it a decorative art? Or is it a new discipline born out of a spark of Modernist passion for 'independent' objects?

If we are to chart this period, we must chart the history of imagination and the history of ambition. We must find a way of charting the grip of imagination for the near East and the Far East, for the places where ceramics can be revivified. We must chart the ambition of where the idea of a single volume could go, how a vessel could become flattened, or multiple, how surfaces could be pitted or scarified. The history of the desire that objects could not be handled, could not be grasped, could be 'unsafe' or make you feel insecure, has yet to be written.

In this history, we should be able to trace the symbiosis between who taught whom and where, of who exhibited with whom, who wrote about whom. And who could not stand whom. A history of animus, a history of regard.

We must ask of this new phenomenon of studio pottery what its ambitions were in the time of Leach, and what they are now. Was it a genuine alternative to industrial ceramic manufacture ('necessary pots')? If so, its expense and technical imperfections were manifest problems. Was it a decorative art, a useful resource for 'interior decorators and architects' to employ (nursery fireplaces, earthenware chargers for country house walls)? Was it an art that was the peer of contemporary painting or sculpture, to be shown in very particular places and ways? Above all there is still work to be done on the Leach inheritance. It remains easier to have Leach as a bugbear, a malign influence strangling the health of ceramics than it is actually to analyse him.

The great, facile polarities that have been set up in ceramic history must be treated more robustly. The expression of oppositional feeling, of the 'abstract vessel' against 'the wheel', of the Mediterranean versus the Orient, the art school versus the workshop are clichés that continue unchecked. The laziness that allows the polarity of handbuilding in opposition to throwing must be revealed. This particular cliché rests on the idea that there is a moral edge that lies in the slowness of handbuilding with its concomitant sense of consideration and fine

judgement. The clichés around throwing pots lie in the immersion in process, the loss of self in repetition.

And we must take on the general feeling amongst potters of *contra mundum,* that the world has set its face against anyone who touches clay, that ceramics are a redoubt to be defended against the ignorant, rather than explained to the interested. Is the great era of manifestos and polemics dead? After Bernard Leach, Michael Cardew, Peter Fuller, David Pye, Peter Dormer, who is going to argue the place for pottery? If we expect manifestos to arrive like New Handiworkers' pamphlets, we will never see what is actually happening. Communication is elsewhere - in internet journals, in seminars, as well as in the letter pages of the newspapers.

In this time of flux between disciplines there are self-evident dangers. But there are also opportunities for realignment in the criticism, and in the curation, of art. The challenges to those who look at, handle, experience art is to find those artists of quality wherever they have chosen to make it. Part of this challenge is to realign our own history, to reveal its richness and complexity.

There's no time left for a craft/art debate.

Michael Cardew, cider jar,
earthenware, 1960s

TEXTILES

Lesley Millar

Craft, design, artisan and art: a short
introduction to studio textile practice since 1970

42

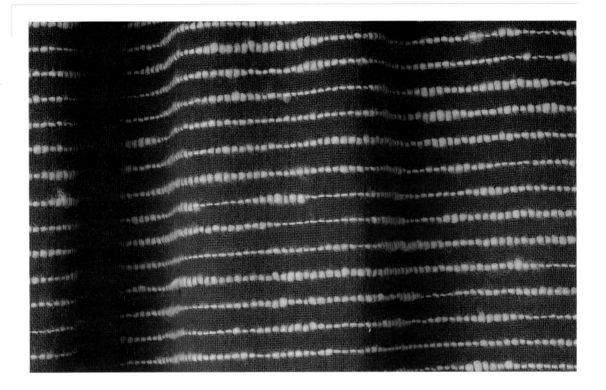

The various approaches to studio produced textiles during the last thirty
years could be seen to illustrate the critical awareness of the position of
craft in an increasingly design conscious consumer environment. Textiles
have played a hugely important role within the emerging craft economy
of the later 20th century, in that as a discipline, textiles move between
fashion, interior design and art. Studio based textile production can
reflect a natural setting and, equally, cutting-edge urban style. The
craft/functional textile has developed alongside the designer led textile,
while the western history of tapestry, with its inherent narrative, has
enabled textile artists to engage with, and contribute to, ongoing
contemporary discourse across a wide range of visual arts.

The textile collection in the Crafts Study Centre catalogues a very distinct
textile genealogy, yet it is fairly safe to assume that at the outset none

Ethel Mairet, handwoven length
of dress material, red cotton,
weft stripes of undyed cheviot
wool, late 1930s

of the early protagonists would have had any idea that they were providing the inspiration for pathways through textile practice in the twentieth century. Ethel Mairet in her workshop in Ditchling and Phyllis Barron and Dorothy Larcher in their studio, first in London and then in the Cotswolds, were all motivated by their fascination with texture, structure, surface, and by their need to maintain a direct hand-eye relationship, and their love of textiles. Their enthusiasm and understanding of their craft drew others into their working environments, and they in turn, taught and inspired the following generation, who then did the same, creating a line which we can follow from the early part of the 20th century to the beginning of the 21st century. It is interesting to note that both pathways, print and weave, lead, via many other influences, to Farnham and The Surrey Institute of Art and Design where those textile practitioners who believe in the values championed by the early pioneers have found a natural place, and where the Crafts Study Centre has now established its home.

In 1972, the Crafts Study Centre held its first exhibition, which contained many textile works from the collection including works by Rita Beales, Ursula Brock, Peter Collingwood, Ethel Mairet, Barbara Mullins, Gwen Mullins, Elizabeth Peacock, Marianne Straub and Harold Summers. 'These people were already recognized as the pioneers, standing for an early twentieth-century revival in the hand techniques of spinning yarn from natural fibres, dyeing with vegetable or organic dyestuffs and weaving in relatively small quantities on hand-looms'.[1] This exhibition was particularly important for textile makers, making visible the outcomes of individual studio/workshops, demonstrating an alternative to the industrial route for the textile designer. At that time there was a strong impetus to connect with this history of textile practice, which had been much concerned with those traditional aspects of textile practice and with a belief in skill and quality. These activities, rooted in a rural environment with ready access to natural materials, came to be synonymous with a nostalgic image of a mythological, more 'authentic', time, characterised by Christopher Frayling as 'The Myth of The Happy Artisan'.[2] This image was hard for those working in textiles to shed, and it was also not an accurate representation of the motivations of those earlier weavers and printers. As Peter Collingwood recalled, Ethel Mairet's:

involvement with other artists and thinkers made her realise that weaving, if it was to have any present-day relevance at all, had to be forward-looking, had to fit into the most modern interior, had to be suitable for the latest fashions. This was the message she was always trying to hammer home; that hand-weaving dealt with the present, that it should be concerned with new materials, be in touch with the newest movements in art and architecture; and that, above all, it was certainly not a delightful and folksy wander down memory lane.[3]

Skill also has 'had a very mixed press within Modernist culture… derided as limiting the potential of mind to generate a truly liberated poetic vision'.[4] Craft textiles are dependant upon the highest level of material understanding, of accumulated skills and knowledge; for skills to be separated from the quality of aesthetic experience would be a denial that the 'material has the potential to be raised into a higher state'.[5]

The 1970s could be typified by the opening out of opportunities for the crafts in Britain, a time in which official recognition was given to contemporary craft activity. In 1973 *The Craftsman's Art,* with over 60 textile exhibits, was shown at the Victoria and Albert Museum, London, reconnecting with the prestigious role that crafts and applied arts once held. This exhibition brought contemporary craftsmen and women to public notice and launched the Crafts Advisory Committee (later to become the Crafts Council). It was also the same year that the Institute of Contemporary Art showed an exhibition of stunning Navajo blankets to critical acclaim. Together these two exhibitions highlighted the directions that studio/workshop based textiles would take over the next years: craft, design and art.

The Sunday Telegraph Craft Awards and other similar initiatives, together with the increasing role of the Crafts Advisory Committee in the financial support and exhibition of contemporary crafts, all increased the public profile of craft, and encouraged aspiring makers to consider craft as a career. This in turn led to a reassessment within art colleges as to the nature of training – should the training for a career as a studio based textile practitioner be different from that for a potential designer for the textile industry? Up until this point, those who wished to be studio-based

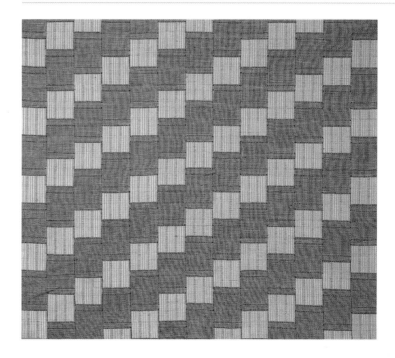

textile makers had trained in the studios and workshops of established weavers and printers. This kind of 'apprenticeship' practice was no longer economically viable and it became apparent that existing degree courses would need to address the new demand, create opportunities for students to have direct experience of the full range of activities in the production of finished cloth. Many colleges were able to develop existing links. For example the traditional carpet industry in Kidderminster provided the motivation for the hand production of all types of floor coverings. West Surrey College of Art and Design (now The Surrey Institute of Art & Design) had always placed individual studio practice at the centre of its courses and the new interest in hand weaving and printing strengthened this approach. The post-graduate course at the Royal College of Art revised its essential requirement 'that a degree had to include six months in industry, to include self-employment (within a studio or workshop) as being "in industry"'.[6]

46

Once qualified, the problem for studio-based practitioners was how to resolve the demands on their time and energies between satisfying the commercial enterprise and their individual creative search. The need to extend knowledge could not always be satisfied by the production of lengths of cloth for clients who might or might not exist. In 1977 the Crafts Advisory Committee, aware of the need to stimulate and make connections with new markets, commissioned seven weavers to make kneelers for seven churches and cathedrals in order to commemorate the Queen's Silver Jubilee. This project brought together weavers Peter Collingwood, Vanessa Robertson and Norman Young who made clear reference to their link with earlier textile practitioners – Elizabeth Peacock, Ethel Mairet, Susan Bosence - along with others, like Roger Oates, who were looking to embrace new links with the design industry. The resulting exhibition demonstrated the inherent potential in the site-specific commissioning practice, which would become so important to many studio-based textile practitioners in the 1980s.

Although it would be incorrect to parcel each decade separately, as obviously there is a continuum from one to the next, in the 1980s the character of the craft world began to change and this was reflected in studio textile practice. Many of the newly qualified textile makers had set up in communal studios situated in metropolitan areas and they were responding in various ways to their urban surroundings. Sally Greaves-Lord, who had studied textiles at West Surrey College of Art and Design during the 1970s, found that living in London changed her work. She began printing primarily with black, using a bleaching out agent to achieve a contrast, and her designs were influenced by the city landscape.[7] The urban environment was also nurturing textile makers whose work was sharp and colourful, who were making connections with the design and art worlds. In 1981 the exhibition *Gaudy Ladies* at the Royal College of Art in 1981 was a celebration of colour, and included the work of tapestry weaver Marta Rogoyska, and ikat weaver Mary Restieaux. Rogoyska was energetic and stylish, her work was humorous and extrovert, using a precise, hard-edged language of colour, material and form. She excelled in commissioned work for architect-designed spaces and helped set the agenda for commissioning practice in the 1980s and 1990s. Restieaux's beautiful, colour-saturated, silk ikat hangings became points of reference for crossover between craft,

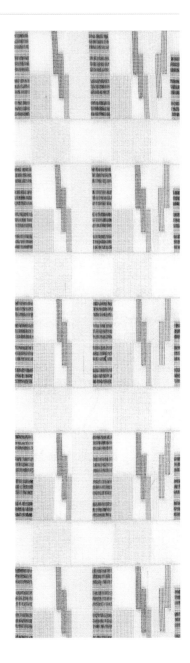

design and art. That her designs could be seen in fashion houses, on wrapping paper and in galleries was an inspiration for some and confused others: 'it was hard to guess what Mary Restieaux's narrow silk hangings could be used for, but they were lovely – intense and fading ikat stripes, luminous and undulating colour'.[8] Restieaux, as a studio-based weaver, was actively looking to make links with industry; Greaves-Lord was also seeking to be more commercial with an intention to employ others to carry out small batch productions. At Kettles Yard in Cambridge, also in 1981, the exhibition *Textiles Today* featured three craft weavers who were attempting to find their place in relation to industry. As one of the participants, Amelia Uden, wrote in *Crafts* magazine: 'the "individual weaver" must have the same choice of materials as the industry – they must have access to fine quality yarns as well as "hand-weaving" yarns and to the same high standard of dyes and finishes seen in the best industrial weaving. Only then will the craft weaver benefit the weaving industry'.[9]

The move towards making links with the design industry was supported by the Crafts Council who, in 1984, organised *Texstyles*. Ten independent textile practitioners developed collections working with fashion or interior designers, manufacturers and retailers. The intention was to encourage studio-based textile practitioners who wished to extend into short-run production and to make the textile and fashion industry aware of the contribution that could be made by independent designer-makers. The textile makers ranged from rug weavers Roger Oates and Fay Morgan, felt maker Annie Sherburne and printers John Chapple and Louise Hamlin Wright. The project was completed with a high profile conference and launch of the outcomes at the Victoria and Albert Museum in London. Opening the conference, Audrey Levy, who had managed the project, explained: 'the specific difficulties encountered by weavers, knitters, printers and embroiderers are largely what initiated this project: difficulties in purchasing yarns, dye stuffs and materials in small quantities at a reasonable price, difficulties in finding UK yarns and material of the quality that people want to use, difficulties in purchasing manufacturing capacity beyond the sample stage. (The latter was perhaps more difficult for the fabric printers than for many of the other participants)'.[10] This initiative made possible a much wider interchange between practitioners, identifying common needs and putting these into

Amelia Uden, textile sample, drawloom-woven, procion-dyed cotton in geometrical block design, 1982

© Amelia Uden/ Crafts Study Centre, 2004

a context which could be supported by a major institution like the Crafts Council. From the perspective of now, it is interesting to note the re-branding of craft practitioners as designer-makers, which became common currency during this time. The hybrid nature of textiles allowed for a flexibility of identity with a wide network of influence, and as already stated, those involved in *Texstyles* were already working in fashion and interior design. However, one result of this re-branding, which we can now identify, was a distancing between the perceived, contemporary, activity of design, and traditional craft practice.

The Crafts Council was committed to addressing issues of making; other issues, emerging through Post-Modern debate, were seen to be less the concern of those engaged in craft practice. By the early 1990s a serious divide had emerged in the crafts between the nature of quality, the value of skill and Post-Modern ironic use of narrative and symbolism. Textiles had become politicised, textile practice was now the site of feminist debate, identified so clearly by Rozsika Parker in *The Subversive Stitch,* first published in 1984, and the exhibition of the same name in 1988. As curator of the exhibition, Pennina Barnett explained: '*The Subversive Stitch* belongs, I think, to a transitional moment. The contemporary exhibition, which I curated, examined the role of textiles in shaping women's social, cultural and individual identities; yet it also sought to destabilise stereotypical assumptions about both women and textiles'.[11] Many individual craft textile practitioners, including Surrey Institute textile graduates Lesley Mitchison and Shelly Goldsmith, winner of the 2002 Jerwood Applied Arts Prize, began to investigate the potential use of textile knowledge and understanding of textile history within contemporary fine art discourse. Mitchison constructed her delicate hand-woven cloth into semblances of corsets. 'A corset speaks to us of use and abuse, of support and constraint. The exquisite craft skills Mitchison brings to her work heighten our awareness of its unspoken history'.[12]

Studio-based craft practice which had, for so long, been defined as being anti-technological was discovering the excitement of new materials and the rise of new technology with a subsequent invigoration of craft textiles. Synthetic fibres were re-branded for the new age: 'Polyamide, a true fibre of the 1990s, is the new name for nylon which, with viscose,

Sally Greaves-Lord
'Underground', silk screen-
printed banner, discharge dyed,
1990s

© Sally Greaves-Lord/
Crafts Study Centre, 2004

dominates the manufacture of the new, revolutionary textiles'.[13] The
investigative work into flexible materials crossed national boundaries and
disciplines. Links between craft, fashion, architecture, engineering and
science were taking place in textile studios. Metal fibres were introduced
into cloth, producing structures, which could be freestanding or drape,
and the 'finishing' of a fabric took on new importance with the
combination of synthetic and natural fibres. The influence of Japanese
innovation grew throughout the decade, with textile planner Junichi Arai
and textile designer Reiko Sudo in the forefront. The company they
jointly founded, NUNO, had a radical approach to cloth instantly
recognisable through the unlikely combination of materials: silk, cotton,

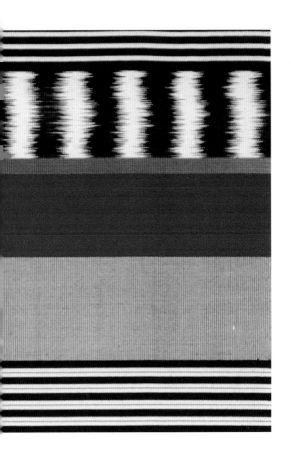

wool, linen, enhanced by the addition of newspaper, copper, stainless steel. Threads with incompatible shrink ratios were intertwined and tossed into a hot dryer to create unprecedented sculptural textiles. In Britain textile practitioners like Frances Geesin, Sophie Roet, Rebecca Earley and Isabel Dodd began to combine new materials, industrial techniques and traditional studio practice. Roet, for example, wove cloth with a mixture of natural and industrial materials, experimenting with silk and phosphorous yarn and a 'wandering' warp and weft technique with a divoré burn-out finish, producing a light-sensitive three-dimensional surface. Geesin was making links, based on her research at the Royal College of Art, with the electronics industry. She was responsible for introducing Philips to conductive fibres and inks, providing the building blocks for their work with wearable electronics. Others weavers - for example, Ann Richards and Philippa Brock - experimented with structure, combinations of materials and finishing processes. Brock's computer aided jacquard weave structures allowed for a cloth flexibility previously more associated with knitted textiles. As the cloth is woven the process of transforming the fibres is set in motion; movement is generated as one type of fibre starts to respond to another. The pleated fabrics woven by Ann Richards use the contained energy inherent in the high twist yarns and the subsequent release of this energy through the wet finishing process to create the finished form of the fabric.[14]

Textile practitioners had placed themselves at the centre of a series of connections across disciplines. Amongst these cross-discipline approaches was the spatial intervention with the built environment in the form of 'architectural' textiles. The western history of tapestry has meant that we are accustomed to hanging textiles on the walls and this tradition was continued and developed during the 1970s and 1980s with tapestry weavers such as Marta Rogoyska and Joanna Buxton, textile printers like Diana Harrison and Sally Greaves-Lord, all making wall-hung work for architect designed spaces. However, other approaches were being explored, ones in which textiles interacted directly with space. Sally Freshwater was one of the first in Britain to use her 'solid training in textiles'[15] to investigate problems of material, scale and space, acknowledging stitch as being: 'very important in understanding the relationship between the thread and the cloth, but it was functional rather than decorative; structure was important'.[16] Again, Japanese

52

approaches to these issues have been remarkably influential. Japan has had a long history of textile practice but no tradition of tapestry. Japanese contemporary textile artists created a new genre of textiles, three-dimensional, free-standing, hung in space, dependent on the highest level of technical and material understanding, always with the intention that the completed work would work in harmony with its surrounding space. Two exhibitions in Britain, one at each end of the decade, *Restless Shadows* in 1991 and *Textural Space* in 2001, were showcases for this Japanese approach to textiles and both exhibitions generated huge amounts of public and specialised interest, particularly in the sound craft base within the work and the experimental spirit.

Now, in the first decade of the 21st century, there is a vastly diverse range of activity being undertaken by studio based textile practitioners, who are constantly rethinking their working methods, looking towards the interdisciplinary approach. These may include the production of a length of cloth involving research into a combination of scientific approach and an understanding of finishing processes, or the development of a textile response as an articulation of space requiring engineering or architectural collaboration. Textile practice continuously divides and grows; the vigour attached to this type of hybridisation creates the energy that ensures its survival. All these approaches are accompanied by a strong imperative to produce work that retains its essential textile identity and is appropriate for its function, whatever that might be. In this respect the link with those early pioneers is still strong. When asked to comment on the emerging debate around craft practice, Marianne Straub replied:

> I suppose a designer and weaver of cloths is a creative craftsman. Why should one be anything else?... It is when these distinctions become important that the work goes wrong, one then has to become clever, different, strident. A length of cloth should be beautiful and serve the purpose for which it was made.[17]

Anne Lander, handwoven shawl, handspun natural grey Shetland fleece, brown cashmere weft c 1982

© Anne Lander/
Crafts Study Centre, 2004

[1] Margot Coatts, 'Thirteen Weavers, A guide to woven textiles in the Crafts Study Centre Collection'. The essay is published on the Arts and Humanities Data Service website, www.ahds.ac.uk.

[2] Christopher Frayling, 'The Myth of The Happy Artisan', *Crafts*, 54 (January/ February 1982) p.17 'The recent "craft revival" is clearly based on a certain reading of English history, using evidence of the aesthetic (as well as moral and ritual) value of certain English artefacts from the past as evidence of how these artefacts must have been both produced and consumed... Most of the "artist craftsmen" or "designer craftsmen" we interviewed have disassociated themselves completely from the popular image of the craftsman... But many of these "artist craftsmen" and "designer craftsmen" - whether they like it or not - belong to a tradition....of giving craftsmanship some respectable origins, and they depend on clients who may be "reacting against" mass-produced goods by investing in well-made, well-designed, scarce domestic objects; these clients may also be reacting against the wilder excesses of Modernism when they decide to own a piece of art which they understand and which is *tangible*'.

[3] Peter Collingwood, 'The Gospel of Weaving', *Crafts*, 64 (September/October 1983) p.22

[4] Ed., Paul Greenhalgh, *The Persistence of Craft* (A&C Black, 2003) p16

[5] op. cit.

[6] Ann Sutton, 'Which Textile Course?', supplement to *Crafts*, 42 (January/February 1980)

[7] Jan Cumming, 'Esprit de corps', *Crafts*, 68 (May/June 1984)p.17
'Life at the Royal College was friendly, but living at Tooting Broadway was grim. Her colours changed. She decided to enforce limitations and to print primarily with black, using a bleaching-out agent to achieve a strong contrast. This enabled her to concentrate on shape and form. Drawings of buildings against landscape, one overpowering the other, are the bases for many designs'.

[8] Review of New Faces exhibition at the British Crafts Centre, John Houston, 'New Faces', *Crafts*, 37 (March/April 1979) p.53

[9] Amelia Uden, 'Plain Weaving', *Crafts*, 50 (May/June 1981) p.33

[10] Report on *Texstyles* conference (Crafts Council, 1984)

[11] Pennina Barnett, foreword to *Revelation*, exhibition catalogue (Kent County Council)

[12] Lesley Millar, *Revelation*, exhibition catalogue (National Museum of Modern Art, Kyoto, Japan)

[13] Sarah E. Braddock and Marie O'Mahony, *technotextiles* (Thames and Hudson) p10

[14] Lesley Millar, *From the Shadow to the Light*, exhibition catalogue (Contemporary Applied Arts, London, 2001)

[15] Sally Freshwater, *Art Textiles of the World - Great Britain, Vol. 2* (Telos Art Publishing) p80

[16] op. cit.

[17] Marianne Straub in conversation with Marigold Coleman, 'A Weaver's Life', *Crafts*, 32 (May/June 1978) p.41

LETTERING

Ewan Clayton

Calligraphy and Lettering in the UK

58

From today's perspective four lettering artists stand out as pioneers of the British twentieth century lettering revival. Edward Johnston laid the practical and intellectual basis for contemporary formal penmanship and its application to different media. Eric Gill, Johnston's student, transferred this understanding into stone cut inscriptional lettering and type design. David Jones, who worked for a time alongside Gill, blended what he saw with his own development as painter and poet to create a new allusive and informal approach to drawn letterform and compositional structure. And Irene Wellington's influence also appears crucial. She managed to show in her own work how Johnston's teaching could form a basis for personal development. Those she influenced most (I think of Donald Jackson and Ann Hechle) have turned out to be amongst the most creative calligraphers of another generation. The work of Edward Johnston and of Irene Wellington forms the bulk of the lettering collection at the Crafts Study Centre.

This personal review essay takes 1970 - the year the Craft Study Centre was first incorporated as a Charity as its starting point. It is startling to see how at that time the influence of the individuals I mention above was still in the process of being defined. Edward Johnston had died in 1944, but it was not until 1971 that his work of a lifetime *Formal Penmanship*[1] was published posthumously. Four years previously the first biography of Eric Gill had appeared.[2] The first retrospective of David Jones's work, at the Tate, was ten years in the future. Irene Wellington was still at work. And on a lighter note: in 1970 books were still printed by letterpress or set by photo composition. Records were vinyl discs. The fastest communication system was the telephone - and my grandparents still hadn't got one. That spring I was packed off to my senior school.

In 1973, Irene completed her final great work *The Bailiffs of Lydd*, and that same year within the Xerox Corporation's Palo Alto Research Laboratory (PARC) in California the first personal computer was developed. No one had any idea this would be so significant.

Lettering would never be the same once the computer became a ubiquitous tool. The invention of a new accessible digital medium would come to require our society to be conscious in new ways about how we communicate with images and the written word. Ultimately the

Thomas Ingmire,
'Calligraphy.. some thoughts'

This work, commissioned for the opening of the Crafts Study Centre by the acquisition committee, consists of nine booklets documenting Ingmire's thoughts on calligraphy as 'illustrated' diaries over a one and a half year period beginning in December 2002. The diary entries are both hand-written and typographic, with printed reproductions and original works. B9 hand made paper from the Iowa Center for the Book, Saunders Mold made paper, Chinese and Japanese sumi inks, gold leaf on gesso.
© Thomas Ingmire/Crafts Study Centre, 2004

ALL OTHER IMAGES (pages 62, 63, 68,69,70,71)
Thomas Ingmire, from
'Calligraphy,...some thoughts'

development of this technology would shake all the institutions evolved over the last five hundred years to bring the world of the written word into order. Libraries, publishing houses, literary genre, copyright law, academia, the postal service, our filing and document processing systems, even the concept of 'authorship' would experience shifts and uncertainty about their identity. In some cases their very existence would be questioned. For five hundred years, since that heady combination of the development of printing and the ferment of the Italian Renaissance there can scarcely have been a more exciting or alarming time to be a lettering artist.

Without realising how fortunate I was, I grew up near Ditchling in Sussex, where two generations of my family worked in the Guild of St. Joseph and St. Dominic founded by Eric Gill. The area was steeped in the history of the early twentieth century craft movement. Mrs Mairet, from whom my grandfather Valentine KilBride had learned weaving, lived in Ditchling. Bernard Leach began writing his *A Potter's Book* there one summer, in a caravan on the Downs. Shoji Hamada and Soetsu Yanagi visited and also in the village lived Edward Johnston. He died twelve years before I was born, but my god-mother was his nurse and my grandmother knew Greta, Johnston's wife, so his presence was still very much felt - he was of course always 'Mr Johnston' never Edward. The first 'real life' calligrapher I met was Irene Wellington. In 1977 she saw a calendar I had made and liked one letter S (I have since realised there were over 900 other obviously unremarkable letters on the sheet!). She asked to meet me. Because I lived near Ditchling I think she felt a responsibility to tell me who Johnston was, to pass something on. It is due to her that I had the courage to follow calligraphy as a career, or rather... a way of life. Irene was also helpful in another way, in 1974, inspired by reading Jung, I had gone to University to be a psychologist but I discovered that I missed working with my hands; Irene showed me how I could put these two influences together!

After University I studied at Roehampton with Ann Camp and worked for a while as her assistant and then by an unusual set of circumstances found myself, in the mid 1980s, at Xerox PARC. There I was a member of a think-tank drawn from many disciplines: anthropologists, philosophers, linguists, historians, computer scientists and typographers.

Our brief was to look at the new digital technology and try to figure it out, our first job was simply to discover how to talk about it! The word we came up with amongst ourselves for describing the products of the personal computer (sound, film, printed paper) was 'document'. It had a slightly awkward legalistic ring then, but now it is the common description. The most interesting part of the work for me was figuring out how we used writing and written communication in the first place, for unless we understood how documents already functioned how could we possibly bring a new technology to bear on the material? Most of the spectacular failures to integrate new technology into workplaces stem from the lack of such careful research into understanding how existing systems actually function. These paper systems are usually wonderfully sophisticated. I still do this kind of work today, though now it is based at the University of Washington in Seattle. So that explains briefly my own nexus with the times.

What of the story of my community, we calligraphers and lettering artists? The 1970s were a difficult time for those wanting an education in calligraphy and lettering, there was virtually none to be had. Since this fact has shaped everything that came after it is worth taking a moment to understand why.

In 1948 Robin Darwin began the reorganisation of the Royal College of Art in order to make it once more a school for designers for industry. Evolving from an idea for a school of 'Typography and Design for Publicity', a school of 'Graphic Design' was established. The challenge for calligraphy was to envision itself allied to commercial art. The American calligrapher Arnold Bank, who worked at the college on a Fulbright Fellowship in 1958/9, had a great impact with his lectures demonstrating the compatibility of calligraphy in this context. Indeed in the USA, from then until now, calligraphers have always worked in a commercial design setting. But as far as calligraphy and lettering are concerned 'publicity design' is just one application of its many applications in a society using the written word. Because for the last forty years 'graphic design' is the only area in art schools to deal with lettering we no longer find this concept of training strange - though we should. To draw a parallel, it is as if architectural education was to be limited solely to the construction of retail outlet: for any other kind of architecture you

just had to work it out for yourself. The calligraphy staff at the Royal College at that time could simply not adjust to this change.

In 1953 calligraphy was closed down as an option at the RCA. The knock on effect was disastrous. A precedent had been set. In the subsequent nationwide reforms of the sixties it was to the Royal College that most Art schools looked for their model of restructuring, here again calligraphy suffered elimination or assimilation into departments of Graphic Design. This assimilation was death by a thousand cuts. The reason was simple, unlike any of the other five subject areas outlined in the Coldstream Report of 1960, Graphic Design was unique in having no designated choice of 'chief studies', a widely spread education in Graphics had to be provided. Within the area of Three Dimensional Design, opportunities were available to study a course with a strong craft base, emphasising unique products and leading to self-employment as a 'studio craftsman'. No such opportunities were available within Graphic Design. From having been a subject that could be specialised in for up to six years, where it did survive, the lettering and calligraphy element, within a three year course, was now confined to a few days. This is still the position today. Not even the rudiments of calligraphy and lettering can be taught in this time. This is the simple answer to explaining why ninety percent of the calligraphy collection at the Crafts Study Centre predates 1960.

But there were other unfortunate effects. Calligraphy as it was at the Royal College in the 50s became frozen in time as the popular image of the subject, at least in the educational world. Several generations of designers and architects were then raised to these prejudices, so markets shrank and work was harder to get. Within the calligraphic community itself these developments precipitated a kind of re-entrenchment making calligraphy in this country smaller minded and more conservative than it would have been if full time educational opportunities had been maintained.

Let me paint the opposite picture for a moment. What would have happened if a full time training in lettering had continued to be available within main stream art education? During the sixties, riding on the back of the abstract expressionists and their links with calligraphy in Japan (I think of artists such as Inoue Yu-Ichi, Toko Shinoda, Franz Kline, Pierre

THE TANNER G

Alechinsky, Pierre Soulanges) Calligraphy might well have moved into the Fine Art Department. There links would also have been made more quickly with the heritage of other calligraphic cultures. Arabic calligraphy, for instance, would have contributed an influence for the sixties saw huge changes in this work as newly independent countries with an Arab heritage sought a basis for art and design free from the influence of a colonial past. Brody Neuenschwander has written about the unacknowledged western tradition of calligraphy within the fine arts. We can cite, Cy Twombly, Mark Toby, Brice Marden, Richard Prince and the Pop artists, David Hockney, Bruce Nauman, Jenny Holzer, Antoni Tapies, Ed Ruscha, Joseph Bueys, John Cage... (the list is in fact endless) they have all used letter forms within their art or been inspired by calligraphic form... what if these connections had been able to be made?

One area survived this institutional collapse because it was not based within the establishment 's institutions but rather in the workshops of practising craftspeople: this was the tradition of letter cutting handed on by Gill and his many apprentices. As brutalistic modernism began to fade as a fashion in architecture these workshops grew. Richard Kindersley worked tirelessly to champion the interests of lettering on buildings, his workshop, and the workshops of his father David, of John Skelton, and others transmitted their skills to new generations. Today this work is one of the most vigorous, young and luxuriant parts of the British lettering tree.

As the lack of educational provision was beginning to be felt in the early 70s the SSI (Society of Scribes and Illuminators) formed in 1921 by two of Johnston's students responded with an expansion of its activities. The society began the publication of a Newsletter, initiated a regular series of workshops, and encouraged the formation of regional groups, thirty-nine

by the end of the eighties, by which date its membership had grown from a little over one hundred in 1970 to well over two thousand. It also began a regular programme of publications of which *The Calligraphers Handbook*[3] remains the high point.

Two courses of some substance did survive the sixties; one led by Anthony Wood at Reigate School of Art and Design with a particular strength in heraldic art, and the course at the City and Guilds run by Berthold Wolpe and Brenda Berman covering a range of applied lettering skills (now closed). Calligraphy courses at the Roehampton Institute were begun by Ann Camp in 1979 specifically as a response to the lack of specialist provision. In 1995 these were converted for a brief period of years into BA courses but are now once more at Certificate and Diploma level - a beneficial move as it allows more time for practical course work. These courses kept calligraphy and hand drawn lettering alive - just. Ann Camp's courses attracted an international group of students from sixteen countries and its influence remains crucial.

My own feeling was that in the 1990s confidence was finally beginning to return to the calligraphy scene. New groups were organised, Letter Exchange provided a forum for calligraphers, typographers and lettercutters to meet, the Calligraphy and Lettering Arts Society was established as was The Memorial Arts Charity. At the end of the 90s the Edward Johnston Foundation was formed. It organised a series of three exhibitions on Handwriting, Calligraphy and Digital Typography and avant-garde calligraphy in a cross-cultural setting. It has continued to organise an annual seminar focussing (but not exclusively) on the intersection between calligraphy and type. In 1999 a new Calligraphy Research Initiative was established at Sunderland University and a calligrapher (it happens to be me!) was appointed as Visiting Professor.

But enough about infrastructure. What about the formal development of the subject? The pages of the 1976 edition of *Calligraphy Today*[4] shows much work that would not have looked out of place in the 1950s but the work of a handful of individuals betrays a new influence. Irene Wellington, Ann Hechle, Stuart Barrie and Alison Urwick show that the more informal compositional style and vernacular Roman forms of painted inscriptions by David Jones had been noticed. This influence

Tom Perkins, gallery sign for the
Crafts Study Centre, carved
Cumbrian slate, 2004

© Tom Perkins/
Crafts Study Centre, 2004

STRANGE TO BEHOLD
IS THE STONE OF THIS WALL
BROKEN BY FATE:

THE STRONGHOLDS ARE BURSTEN·
THE WORK OF GIANTS DECAYING·
THE ROOFS ARE FALLEN
THE TOWERS TOTTERING·
MOULDERING PALACES ROOFLESS·
WEATHER MARKED MASONRY
SHATTERED SHELTERS
TIME SCARRED·TEMPEST MARRED
UNDERMINED OF OLD
EARTH'S GRASP HOLDETH
ITS MIGHTY BUILDERS
TUMBLED CRUMBLED
IN GRAVEL'S HARD GRIP:
TILL A HUNDRED GENERATIONS
OF MEN PASS AWAY

would grow over the years and today nearly every lettering artist has these forms in their visual imagination. Some, I think of Tom Perkins and Hazel Dolby are notable in having transformed their work into something recognisably their own. Tom Perkins in particular has matured into a letterer (and calligrapher) who can hold his own with anyone in our very long tradition.

Another new strand in that survey is the presence of work by Karl Georg Hoeffer, Freidrich Poppl, Hermann Zapf, Freidrich Neugebauer and, from the former Hansa trading town of Tallin, Estonia, Villu Toots. This German influenced presence represents a post war rapprochement for two great traditions which, prior to the second world war, had many close connections. The politicisation of lettering in Germany just before the war and the effects of the war itself interrupted this dialogue which resumed in the 1970s. But the mark of the experience of the '30s is evident in the choice of forms these calligraphers developed. Turning their back on their immediate historical base they draw on rhythmical handwriting, the use of the brush rather then the pen and elegant Renaissance, lightly weighted, Roman Capitals, the personification of sophisticated balance and poise. These themes are much in evidence also in the 1998 edition of *Calligrapghy Today* where we can see them being picked up in the work of David Howells (the first English calligrapher, as far as could see from their visitor book, to visit the Klingspor Museum in Offenbach where the greatest collection of twentieth century German calligraphy is held), and in work by Tom Perkins and Gaynor Goffe. German work would have an even wider impact in the USA after the teaching visits made there by Hermann Zapf, Karl Georg Hoeffer and latterly Gottfried Pott during the 1980s and 1990s.

Today the single most important overseas influence on English speaking calligraphers is probably the Berliner, Hans Joachim Burgert. Isolated in West Berlin he developed his own rigorously analytical approach to letterform based on his training as an abstract artist under Karl Schmidt-Rottluff and Ernst Schumacher. He first visited Britain in the 1980s where I remember the excitement in the room as he gave his talk and we realised that for the first time we were hearing a genuine, well thought through, alternative to our own understanding of form. But the beauty of it was that it was not in opposition to our perspective but

March 6, 2003

In San Francisco there currently is a calligraphy study group that meets each month at the public library to look at works from the Harrison Calligraphy Collection. The focus frequently is on typography or if not, it is on the typographic view of calligraphy that I have previously discussed. Skill of the maker and perfectly formed letters are the other most admired attributes. There is little or no discussion of content– whether something is worth doing– or on the relationship between what a work says and what it looks like. This is not uncommon in calligraphic circles. I don't mean to be critical of my colleagues. Somehow I do want more from them, but most of all I want more from myself. The difficult part for me is the discussion that emerges when something is "illegible." It never begins or even gets to the point of accepting that a work has value when it cannot be read. The merit of a work, its truth, its beauty, its mystery, its magic, never gets explored. It is just "illegible."

The curious thing is that very few calligraphers ever read the works that they insist must be legible. They do admire the letterforms, the composition, and the richness of the materials. On one level the admiration seems to be for the human skill that can reach the perfection of the machine, and on the other, praise is given to the qualities (particularly of the materials) that can only be created by hand. Legibility really is not the issue–

rather the concerns are for letter forms, from a fairly narrow perspective, and craft skills. Creativity and the spirit that drives it, are "short-changed."

At the heart of the matter, I do not believe that calligraphy has anything to do with whether a text can be read. At the same time it has everything to do with writing and the spirit of writing as opposed to, say, drawing or painting. Writing, whether it can be read or not– or perhaps when it cannot be read– is the thing that links cultures and civilizations. It expresses the timeless human desire to say "I am"– to make the mark that identifies oneself as both an individual and as a member of civilization. We feel that connection when we see images form the early cave picto-picto, or when we look at writing in medieval manuscripts, or read our grandparent's letters, or see our children's first a, b, c's. Writing has a truth; our challenge as calligraphers, supposedly the masters of writing, is to find it. I believe that if calligraphy is to have meaning it must be an honest expression of its maker. And the "maker" must also somehow stand separate from the crowd. This has nothing to do with the function of transcription (communication by words). "Writings' truth," in the words of Roland Barthes, "is in the hand which presses down and traces a line, i.e. in the body which throbs (which takes pleasure)"... "for writing to be manifest in its truth (and not in its instrumentality), it must be illegible."

complementary to it, capable of extension to the latest developments. The reason his thought (circulated through typescript, exhibitions of work and lectures) was so well received in Britain was I think precisely because Johnston's careful analytical approach had prepared us to think about form analytically. In the hands of calligraphers such as Brody Neuenschwander and Thomas Ingmire, Burgert's influence has given a new breath of life to letter form and composition.

In my own view there is one further strand we need to add to our discipline to enable it to stand on its own feet in our time and that is a

January 04, 2003

THE VISUAL/VERBAL PROBLEM This image by Christian Dotremont, a Belgian artist who was a part of the COBRA movement in Europe, has been quite provocative to me for a very long time. The work is obviously writing but gives emphasis to the visual message of the words rather than to the verbal reading of the words. The levelled letterforms and their presentation by Dotremont makes the French poem virtually unreadable: although, when one knows the poem, it is possible to begin the decipher some of the words. To read the words of the poem clearly is not the objective of the work. To "see" the poem in the way one "sees" a painting or a drawing is more to the point. Dotremont acknowledged his interest in the visual by presenting readable versions of the texts along with his visual impressions.

Visually this work places emphasis on the interaction between the figure and the ground (the black marks of the letters and the white shapes that they make). This interplay between figure and ground was a common theme of the works by the Abstract Expressionists. The volumes of the white shapes in opposition to the the black sign create a balanced tension which makes the white active against the black: in many places the white shapes actually appear to emerge from the black—creating the sense of a pulsating image of white light. The image is in fact visually expressive of the poem's meaning which is about the the variations in the light that one experiences in the winter landscape. This connection between the visual image and the meaning of the words is significant as a measure of the work's success as well as insightful as a means for understanding the idea of expressive calligraphy.

DOTREMONT POEM

Si neiexa' que soit dans l'Extreme Nord l'Ouest et si sendee tout soit la nuit que nous venions épaisis entoure si cette nuit, nous y trouvions aussimachiné de luminosities, même date du éclat du ciel, rest, proche, sa de la terre indiscaver neigeuse, ou d'une neuque aurais humide que dans la sensation probablement indéfrouisable de rien tout ce que nous voyions et plus. 1974, Christian Dotremont. Indian ink on paper. *61 x 59 cm, unsigned and undated*

more embodied approach to our work. Here work with musicians, actors and dancers could help. The decision at the annual conference at Sunderland in 2003 to include Christopher Leith, mask maker and puppeteer, in the teaching team was in my view a breakthrough. I also feel that Japanese and Chinese calligraphers have a great deal to teach us on this subject. The influence of avant-garde Japanese calligraphy is a growing influence in the west and as interest in western calligraphy continues to grow in Japan and more western calligraphers travel to teach there, this can only deepen.

Lack of commitment to content or text is still the Achilles heel of western lettering in all areas. Ian Hamilton Finlay has challenged this with the work he has commissioned and Brody Neuenschwander has also drawn attention to this area by his recent description of himself as a 'text artist' - this is one way forward. Another could be a commitment to the life of the communities we live in such a way that we find our work in the supply of written artefacts that help those communities or individuals celebrate what they hold be significant; enabling them to focus their grieving, to remember and validate, witness, and mark significant moments in their home-making or life's pilgrimage. This means thinking up new kinds of artefacts and considering the nature of the rituals in whose care their meaning would rest.

Slowly lettering artists and calligraphers are engaging with the opportunities of new digital technology, using it either as a design tool (as in Donald Jackson's great Bible project for St. John's, Collegeville, Minnesota) or in its own right as a means of showcasing work in CD format or on the web. Few have let the technology influence their forms though Denis Brown is one exception (in the backgrounds to his glass pieces), as is Tom Kemp, and in fairness I should probably mention my own work from the 1990s onwards that has either used the mouse and simple graphics software to draw letterforms directly on screen or has incorporated such new forms back into hand drawn lettering.

The two most exciting happening in the UK at the time of this writing are the works of a lifetime flowing from the pens of Donald Jackson and Ann Hechle. Donald's work is a massive handwritten and illuminated Bible, a project costing many millions of dollars and being produced by a team he has gathered together internationally but based mostly around his home near Monmouth in Wales. It shows the British Calligraphic revival come of age and rivals anything in the long history of western manuscript production. It has been made to be used. Ann Hechle's work, ultimately destined for a home with the Edward Johnston Foundation in Ditchling, is a work on sacred geometry and the design process written in her own words and now in its fifth year of making.

Seeing new work is vital to the long term growth and development of calligraphy - so the fact that the Crafts Study Centre itself has commissioned work for the opening of the new building at Farnham is very much to be welcomed. In the years ahead the balance of its collection needs to be addressed. The massive gap from the 1960s to the present day must be bridged and new technology embraced. The challenge of course is to do this carefully picking out the genuine flow of influences and forms and not to react to the gap with panic by starting something completely different or in opposition to it. This is why I welcome in particular the new commission for Thomas Ingmire, originally a student of Donald Jackson's, but now resident in the USA and one of the most influential of contemporary calligraphers. Calligraphic culture is now global and if the true nature of the impact and growth of the twentieth century revival in lettering and calligraphy is to be recorded, this fact will need increasingly to be recognised.

[1] Ed. Heather Child, *Formal Penmanship* (Lund Humphries, 1971)

[2] Robert Speaight, *The Life of Eric Gill* (Methuen, London, 1966)

[3] Ed. Heather Child, *The Calligrapher's Handbook* (A&C Black, London, 1985)

[4] Ed. Heather Child, *Calligraphy Today* (Studio Vista, London, 1976)

WORDS VS. IMAGES - CONTENT VISUAL - CONTENT VERBAL

Dual Letter composition, 2001 Yumi Tohyama

Detail, Quotations from Mao Zedong, 2000 (Square Word Calligraphy) Xu Bing

FURNITURE

Matthew Burt

The role of the Crafts Study Centre in

defining craft furniture

My early years were charged with a simplistic duality. The outside world, where I purposely roamed the wide horizons of Wiltshire, and the inside world where I slunk through the corridors of academe. That outside world seemed safer with a penknife and baler twine in pocket. All the better to fashion and strap together a sometimes practical and a sometimes fanciful structure, with which to face or pass the day. These structures were made from readily available materials gleaned from hedgerows and coppice. They were assembled with seemingly innate processes and facilitated with primitive tools. The inner world led into the biology of the hedgerow and coppice, the mechanics of their materials and the reasoning behind my structures. My efforts in the outside world seemed to be more successful if oiled with the explanations, formulas and answers provided by the inside world.

While taking refuge from the world in the kitchens and barns of various farming relatives, I learnt to trust the creaking of the Windsor chair as a message of its ability to cope with my antics, rather than the alarm call of imminent collapse. These pieces, burnished by use, seemingly designed by everyman and honed by the repeated perfections of their makers, were to me a revelation of collaboration between thought, knowledge of materials and manipulative skills. They appeared to be symbolically linked to a brightly coloured ribbon of endeavour that undulated into the past, each generation adding to it their discoveries and their times. Their language fascinated me, talking as it did of thought and action, unfettered by fashion or whimsy, a sound starting point, an attitude.

The starting point of the Crafts Study Centre's (CSC) furniture collection is rooted in country furniture, as re-affirmed by the thinkers and makers of the Arts and Crafts Movement. This brings with it a dilemma inherent in its name. Today crafts means many things to many people and the road is littered with the casualties of those who have claimed it for a particular orthodoxy. The CSC selectors risked injury on that same road. Bravely or rashly they thrust their standard in the ground and loudly exclaimed their attitude. It ignored more than it included and could be said to be defined by those omissions. Where is Mackintosh whose influence reverberated through the proto-Modernists? Where are examples of the rigour expressed within the Bauhaus and its allies?

Before I go on to chart where their attitude led them it may be informative if I give you a bit more of mine.

It's back to that childhood duality, or more accurately its demise at the hands of a seething plurality, part of which led me to study zoology. It was here that I met my Professor of Design: a relentlessly uncompromising despot, ruthlessly logical and infinitely open minded, called Natural Selection. Its structures were honed by the repeated perfections of its makers into succinctly adapted objects. The ultimate combination of intelligent use of materials, 'experience', 'knowledge' and 'thought' and tested to destruction in extreme conditions. The end result might be a feather. This could be pure white or an iridescent blue green, flecked with silver circled golden spots, but beneath its surface decoration remains a perfectly designed engine of flight. Most furniture is playing around with the surface decoration or re-arranging the barbs on the shaft of that feather, in response to fashion, individual whim or client pressure. Very few pieces will demonstrate the design leap of mutation and present us with a re-worked feather that is more energy efficient, less material rich and having within it the mathematics of aesthetics. Very few designers can lay claim to having contributed a mutation to the design history of furniture. It is a lifetime's privilege to attempt to discover such a mutation.

Initially, the collection concentrated upon the triumvirate of the Cotswold School, Ernest and Sidney Barnsley and the shining star of the group Ernest Gimson. It is interesting to investigate if their attitudes led to any mutative contributions. Their reaction to late Victorian excess and the vulgar expression of its wealth, coupled with their perception of the dehumanising effects of mass production, led them to seek solace, and inspiration, in the far flung corners of the Cotswolds. They found a clearly identifiable architectural style from farming communities and their associative, supportive and distributive businesses. The tools and implements used in these businesses were still fabricated by local craftsmen using local materials in response to everyday needs. These practical solutions often sported the signature embellishments of the individual hand that made them. The group made an intentional attempt to reconnect to that brightly coloured ribbon of country furniture. Did they succeed? Did they manage to improve the feather?

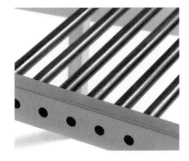

There is one design that I feel comes close, the brave reworking of a traditional ladderback chair by Ernest Gimson. Trusting his makers and his own knowledge of material he bravely created a precarious balance between component failure and delivery of function. Their material of choice was ash, renowned for its pliant, flexing capabilities It was often the traditional timber of choice in chair making. Gimson stripped the chair down to its thinnest, most delicate sections to a point where the chair could be lifted with one finger, yet still survive the ample physique of wealthy clients. Perhaps this chair is an example of the evolutionary leap of mutation. Maybe that it is even worthy of the title 'He made evolutionary climax', too perfect to challenge. The chairmaker Neville Neal made around two hundred of these chairs every year of his working life producing a sublimely balanced chair, honed to perfection by the repetition of his making. His son Peter continues the tradition.

Over the working life of Edward Barnsley, son of Sidney, the shirt tails hanging out of the suitcase of the Arts and Crafts Movement became increasingly difficult to stuff back in. His working life began helping to construct the now famous memorial library at Bedales School in Hampshire, a school that he attended. Under the green oak roof that Edward youthfully clambered over during its construction, can be seen the Arts and Crafts philosophy brought to life. Sidney Barnsley's hayrake tables and Gimson's ladderback chairs are seen in resplendent serried ranks, basking in the warm oak light, and overhung by the exposed honesty of its roof and gallery. Incidentally, the Gimson chairs were manufactured by Edward Gardiner, whose work can be seen within the collection.

Edward Barnsley went on to found his own workshop in nearby Froxfield. Here he bravely wrestled with the legacy of Arts and Crafts roots and its innate contradictions. Many of its principles were swathed in sentiment, determinedly isolationist and uncompromisingly reactionary, locked into an inevitable cul-de-sac. The daring simplicity of Gimson's chair or Sidney Barnsley's hayrake table were increasingly difficult to manufacture economically without the benefit of mass production techniques. They might well be sublime but they were labour intensive and thus only available to the minority that would literally buy over the odds into the ethos. Edward Barnsley's response was slowly to take the furniture away from its country roots and back towards the urbane fineness of line and virtuosity associated with Georgian furniture. Undoubtedly the workshop kept alive and improved a tradition of superb craftsmanship. Its organisation and apprenticeship scheme spawned another generation of makers, who in turn find their place in the collection.

Sandy MacKilligin and Alan Peters have both founded their own workshops. The reactive pendulum has swung again with Alan Peters's work in particular, resolutely demonstrating a lifetime designing and making in pursuit of a pure distillation of form and function. His work combines exquisite craftsmanship with knowledge of materials and the results have delighted clients and students alike.

The roots of the Crafts Study Centre's collection's origin and its attitude are clearly expressed throughout but it also demonstrates the paucity of what might be described as 'craft furniture'. By the time the 1960s arrived such practice was very much on the back foot, seven eighths of the way down a cul-de-sac and reaping the results of its obstinately held orthodoxies. Only a handful of people kept good practice alive. The remainder were either blind, blinkered or ignorant of the excitement boiling in other areas of furniture making which was undergoing a revolution as new materials, new techniques and new thought combined to give genuine evolutionary leaps. What were they missing?

It's time, once again, to go back into that seething plurality. Whilst reeling under the blows of my despotic Professor of Design I took respite in the convoluted, interconnected pathways of Ecology. Ecologists observed in the late 1960s that the greater number of different species that coexisted in an ecosystem, the greater the stability of that ecosystem. The multiplicity of different species and their effects upon each other, and the environment, created checks and balances within the ecosystem, to the point that no one species could dominate or monopolise. This observation was encapsulated in the adage 'diversity leads to stability'.

The CSC collection does not attempt to catalogue the diversity apparent in furniture making of the 20th century. It lights upon a gossamer thin line and illuminates it as an orthodoxy or guide. Within it are some influential designer makers but it is more notable for the absence of significant design advances. It demonstrates the attitude of its selectors and their view that craft furniture is a narrow and specific part of 20th century furniture. I believe that this viewpoint was shattered by the onset of that seething plurality manifested by the explosive interest in designer made furniture that emerged in the late 1960s and early 1970s. The phenomena can only be understood by a comprehension of the meiotic recombination of thought and practice instigated by the social, philosophical and environmental changes associated with those times.

In addition to these changes the Danes swept through the British furniture market during the 1960s. They had successfully married their craft based roots with an intelligent design ethos, facilitated by efficient production methods incorporating both hand and machine techniques. Their economic and elegant results spot lit the lumpen crudity of many of their British counterparts. It also spot lit the blinkered romance and obdurate isolationism of much of British craft furniture. The Danes had successfully linked their craft to design by collectively exhibiting furniture from craft based workshops, to opinion formers and industry. They

caught the attention of both, and persuaded their government and the Danish people that good design, good craftsmanship, good manufacturing techniques and good marketing were a worthwhile investment. Like the Viking invasions of old, they swept all before them.

The British industry was locked into post war austerity. It exhibited the now familiar distrust of creative types. It was cautious, conservative and dull. It was philosophically unsophisticated and hidebound. The maelstrom of creative change raging around it was passing the majority by. Meanwhile creative talent was feeding on an exciting dish, its ingredients made up of political, sociological seismic change. Applied arts and the performing arts were in freefall, bouncing off and newly liberated from, old constraints. Added to the dish was the rhythmic reappearance of idealistic romanticism, akin to that of the Arts and Crafts Movement. The creative cauldron was bubbling furiously, heated by the superb system of arts and design courses offered by the art colleges of that time and stoked by imaginative tutelage. It was not long before the creative potage boiled over, but with few places to go except solo.

Those designers who pursued their curiosity as far as the Royal College of Art were fortunate enough to find Professor Pye as their guide and mentor. David Pye was uncompromisingly intellectual in his approach. He demanded that design thought be central to and inform making practice. His own work is represented within the collection and at first sight may appear contradictory. The work chosen could be described as bowls or platters, their surfaces fluted with the delicate brush strokes of a gouge. This is achieved by the use of an ingenious if bulky carving machine of his own invention (there are examples in the collection). Its elaborate construction gave Pye his preferred mechanical solution. The same delicate flutes could be achieved by the skilled hand wielding a sharp gouge. This neatly demonstrates that similar conclusions can be achieved by different routes and it brings parity to those routes, the two skills held in equal regard and equal acclaim in pursuit of the same goal. The intellect required to invent and realise Pye's carving machine requires a long incubation. The skills necessary deftly to apply the gouge with the hand require a similar incubation. Both defer to their chosen medium of wood, attempting to display something of its essence. Pye's bowls resonate with a distillation of function that reflect that essence.

Gordon Russell, carver, yew c 1931, made for Robin and Heather Tanner

Are they rearranging the colours on the feather or investigating a new engine of flight?

It is not surprising that along with many of Professor Pye's students others coincided in their conclusions. Their view was that the route between idea and object in the industry was labyrinthine and tainted with insurmountable issues that did not address their own concerns. Rewarding placements in the industry were rare. How sweet then the individual who could both design and make. The route between idea and object looked tantalisingly short. However, the hunger to acquire both design and making skills was very difficult to satisfy. There were then, as now, diminishing options and cultural prejudice towards courses specialising in making skills. Then, as now educational administrators were reaching the conclusion that the passing on of practical skills was material rich, space rich, machinery and tool rich, time rich and expensive. The apprenticeship was becoming uneconomic and unfashionable. There were very few options. A handful of publicly funded courses and a similarly sparse number of privately funded courses were hugely oversubscribed. The daunting paucity of opportunity was an obstacle, laboriously clambered over by a growing number of people, fuelled by the idealism and philosophy of those times.

Two alumni of the RCA surmounted that obstacle course. They were among David Pye's early intake of students. They both obviously benefited from his fresh vigour. Both have their work represented in the collection. Richard la Trobe-Bateman's stripped down, fiercely logical stick chairs influenced a new generation of designer makers searching for a rigorous core. His lateral reworking of the refectory table with its triangulating truss support for Pembroke College, Oxford is definitely a consummate redesigning of the feather. David Colwell inspires me to go back to that creaking Windsor chair, the one that was seemingly designed by everyman, honed by the repeated perfections of its makers. There it remains, smugly assured in its evolutionary climax protected from change by its tradition. It took emigration to the New World, the use of a new timber, hickory, and touches of colonial irreverence to move it on to a lighter more delicately elegant structure. It took the design intuition and intellect of David Colwell to impart the Windsor chair with his big bang mutation. He took the steam-bent hoop of its back and

continued its raked angle forward to the floor. He counterbalanced this with two steam-bent back struts angled in the opposite direction to the floor. He linked the two elements with a cantilevered seat supporting strut. The result is a genuine new engine of flight, succinct, appropriate and responsible in its use of materials, quick and energy efficient in its manufacture and aesthetically delightful.

These are rare examples of designer makers whose work has gone beyond rearranging surface decorations or shuffling components. The work springs from an intimate knowledge of, and engagement with, material. In the case of Colwell's chair the material used is ash, a timber also used in Gimson's chair. It is worth a brief aside on the specific qualities of the three stalwarts of British timber, ash, oak and elm as demonstrated in the now rare craft of the wheelwright. The wheel is another object seemingly designed by everyman and honed by the repeated perfections of its makers. The hubs were made from elm, a good choice. Anyone who has repeatedly wielded the axe will know that the interlocking, every-which-way grain makes for a very strenuous pastime: it does not split easily. The spokes were made from riven oak, renowned for its rigid, robust strength through which sailors will vouch, extreme forces can be transmitted. The felloes (outer rims, hooped with iron) were made from ash chosen for its pliant toughness and ability to absorb flex and shock.

Along with Professor Pye's students a plethora of individuals clambered over the obstacles placed in their way to become designer makers. Together, they not only revitalised craft furniture they took it to every conceivable corner of the furniture making spectrum. They explored its barren and fruitful nooks and crannies from traditional country furniture through industrial, corporate, contract, metaphorical, sculptural to conceptual forms. The intellectual rigour of the RCA has already been mentioned. Alumni of various colleges, and here I must mention those of John Makepeace's Parnham, have delighted us with their dexterity and diversity. Alan Peters has influenced a whole generation towards a Cotswold School tradition, which still reverberates. Even the hard to come by apprenticeship has thrown up some rare talent.

The ecologist within me smiles at the witnessing of such vibrant, healthy diversity bringing with it equilibrium of checks and balances where no one orthodoxy is in the ascendant, stifling others with its mono-cultural viewpoint. The designers and makers that emerged in the 1970s and 1980s and their followers in the '90s and beyond have redefined craft furniture probably by rejecting it as a definition. They were helped by the communication and new technology revolutions and mentored by good teaching and the spirit of their times. They have grappled with new materials, new techniques and new thoughts. They have created an atmosphere of an excitement of possibilities. The assertion that design is a central tenet of making practice has been reaffirmed and strengthened to the point that the title 'designer maker' has become acceptable.

What have they achieved? Initially the most noticeable effects came from the boisterous school of makers. Their virtuoso swoops and flights of fancy gamely shuffled the components and dazzled with their decorative effects. Their work ranges form the vulgar to the witty. It is the side of craft furniture that is most populist in appreciation, demonstrating, as it undoubtedly does, a staggering mastery of making.

It infuriates the purist and inspires a compensatory retort from others within designer making.

Within production furniture there has been an almost unseemly scramble to recruit designers. Their collaborative response to new materials, new techniques and new thought has resulted in a torrent of quality product on our high streets, often at accessible prices. The product is often highly crafted, succinct, and appropriate and demonstrates a responsible attitude and interpretation of materials. The work is socially useful, practically and aesthetically functional. Their products put us all on our mettle. However, the route from idea to object is still tortuous and labyrinthine, and with vested interests, is only open to a very small number of designers. Amongst those designers are a number who have emerged from, or remain within, the pragmatic duality of design and making. They retain a directness, flexibility and independence that allows experimentation and personal risk in the tradition of all those Victorian craftsmen/proto engineers who often against insurmountable odds, and fired on by personal belief, brought their product to the benefit of us all.

Much of the more interesting work is emanating from these designer makers on the fringe of industry, redefining and recycling the research thrown up by it and in some cases leading that research. The discipline of its constraining remit, overlaid with the guiding principles of modernism combine with the designer maker's relationship between the intellect and knowledge of materials to deliver succinct, appropriate and beautiful objects. Their results are clearly related to the distillations of the best Arts and Crafts practice.

There are others, who in the tradition of Pye's platters seek a purer language of aesthetics, which I pompously describe as the mathematics of aesthetics. They seem to be seeking an emotional response to the essence of their material. The work of Jim Partridge and his partner Liz Walmsley spans the period from the early days of the collection to today. It represents an uncompromisingly fascinating journey of exploration. Their forms are like wood talking. Another, whose work represents a similar search, is Guy Martin. Gleaning material from hedgerow and coppice in a gentle, environmentally light-footed manner, his work takes me back to my childhood ramblings.

Within best practice today can be glimpsed that brightly coloured ribbon undulating into the past, representing a vigorous, uncompromising, hard nosed attitude towards redesigning that feather and improving it as an engine of flight, sometimes expressing its very essence. It is ironic that there are many who would be embarrassed to have the word 'craft' prefix their discipline, so tainted has the word become. Yet all would be proud to have their results demonstrate truth to material, quality of material, appropriateness of function be that practical, aesthetic, symbolic, metaphorical or conceptual and to be described as showing craftsmanship. Within that irony lies the redefinition of craft furniture. There are those who would take it towards art, perhaps to increase its perceived value, and there is indeed art within it, but I am content to see it down there, where craft has been for millennia, in the dirt of the market place. It has undergone a meiotic recombination with others and itself in a natural reactive rhythm. It has evolved neither into the property of a particular group, nor the preserve of any particular orthodoxy. Rather, it remains an intangible ethos or attitude reverberating around our lives. Its balance of intuition, intellect and body is invigoratingly alive.

CONTEXT

Simon Olding

'A conglomeration of interesting objects':
the significance of the Crafts Study Centre

90

The principal characteristic of the craft infrastructure, from process through to presentation, is the modest size of most ventures. The majority of makers work on their own, or in small teams. Craft galleries are mostly contained within the wider spaces of museums. Commercial craft shops are generally small. Museum curators and exhibition providers achieve a great amount with slender resources and tiny staff numbers. This picture is as true today (2004) as it was in 1970 when the Crafts Study Centre was formed as a charitable trust. The sense of vulnerability and risk in the venture had been present from the outset. Muriel Rose, a founder Trustee, commented in her notes from the meeting of craftspeople and educationalists held in 1967 that:

> there is at present no permanent collection in Great Britain where the work of outstanding artist-craftsmen of our own century may be seen. In order therefore that work of the highest quality may be freely accessible for enjoyment and study, it is proposed to bring together such a collection'.[1]

Innovation (building a unique collection) and risk (for which no substantial resources of funding or space were identified) were yoked together in the concept of this Crafts Study Centre. Robin Tanner bound together into 'two huge volumes' the 'vast record of Barron and Larcher's work', creating an iconic museum object in the process. In doing so 'there was a cry on all sides that this important and beautiful work should not be dispersed, and that examples by other great artist-craftsmen of this century should be rescued and gathered together before it was too late'.[2]

This kind of rescue-scholarship has been the starting point of many great museum collections and many independent museums from the 19th century onwards. The tenacity of the group of makers and educationalists who formed the first Board of Trustees[3] meant that, at one level, space was secured, collections built up through remarkable gifts and the occasional inspired purchase, and funds raised. The concept of the Centre, as a quiet place for study and enjoyment, and a place where materials could be studied at first hand, as well as in the context of thoughtfully presented exhibitions, was hard won. The central role of the Holburne Museum and the University of Bath as the first and key partners in this enterprise cannot be underestimated. They gave the collection both a home, and hope for progress.

Caroline Sharp, willow piece for
the exterior of the Crafts Study
Centre, 2004

© Caroline Sharp/
Crafts Study Centre, 2004

But there was more to the founding vision than this. The first pioneer curator-trustees were motivated by the urgent need to save material both for what it was, and for what it meant. They had a symbolic purpose, too. Safeguarding collections in trust meant more to the founders than building up an attractive and historically rich group of craft objects. They believed that they were also safeguarding and cherishing the spirit of craft practice and process. The assembly of an iconic collection of craft objects also safeguarded, and gave life to, the tradition of making. It is no accident that this purpose was delivered by makers and educationalists. Professional curatorship followed later (with the key appointment of Barley Roscoe). The combination of practitioners and curator saved and developed a significant collection of work by craft pioneers, gathered together before it was lost or forgotten.

Doing this in 1970 was, if anything, harder than attempting to do it in 2004. It was to take another seven years before the Crafts Study Centre opened at the Holburne Museum. Craft collections in the museum sector were marginal. The Crafts Advisory Committee (the precursor to the Crafts Council, becoming known as the Crafts Council in 1979) was only set up in 1971 to administer the government grant to the crafts. There were clear similarities between the two organisations. Both collections were overseen in the main by makers, although the scope of the Crafts Council's collections became wider. The Crafts Study Centre developed a key interest in adding practitioner's archives. The breadth of the collection of images of work selected by 'a committee of master craftsmen'[4] appointed by the British Crafts Centre, grant aided by the Crafts Advisory Committee, demonstrated this wider scope. (Lack of finance, matched with a feeling for the 'essential' probably accounted for the concentration of the Crafts Study Centre on collecting in five principal areas: textiles, ceramics, lettering and calligraphy, wood and furniture and archives. The charitable deed of the Centre gives a longer list of subject areas for potential collection).[5]

A reading of the early Trustee papers (held in the Centre's archives) makes it clear that the activity and aspirations were focused, perhaps inevitably, on the issues of housekeeping and accommodation, as well as the gradual increase in the collections. A programme of exhibitions and publications also gathered momentum during the 1970s, with the highly

significant launch exhibition *20th Century Craftsmanship* held at the Holburne Museum in 1972. The exhibition brought sharply into focus the range and depth of the founding collections, and acted as a stimulus both for wider public appreciation of the Centre, and as a magnet for additional collections.[6] The inaugural exhibition led to an inspired, thoughtful series of shows, curated by the Centre's remarkable and indefatigable founder-curator, Barley Roscoe, and included, for example, *Hand block printed textiles: Phyllis Barron and Dorothy Larcher* (1979), and retrospectives of the work of the weaver Rita Beales (*Flax and Fleece*), and the potter Katharine Pleydell-Bouverie in 1980. All three exhibitions reflected major bodies of work held in the Centre's permanent collections.

The 1970s saw the Crafts Study Centre beginning to find its true voice, as a collection-based focus for research, study and enjoyment. It became a meeting-place for makers and curators, and craft practitioners were central to the delivery of its programme. An acquisition committee, set up in 1981 governed the addition of material into the permanent collections, with sensitivity and scrupulous attention to the quality of work its watchwords.[7] The steady flow of exhibitions was matched by scholarly research into the collections, often with the support of external funds to appoint project authors. A survey of the major museum collections of crafts in 1976 had identified only a modest number where activity was ongoing: the 20th century ceramic holdings at the Victoria & Albert Museum; the Henry Rothschild collection at Bristol City Art Gallery and the Milner-White bequests at York and Southampton. The craft collections of the British Council were first assembled by Muriel Rose in the 1940s, had been 'reaprraised' in the 1960s with systematic collecting only starting again from the 1980s onwards. But the pace of change was slow. An editorial in *Crafts* magazine noted:

> there are also other factors working against the growth of craft collections in museums. In many there is a conglomeration of interesting objects but an atmosphere of confusion prevails over the reason for their presence... Most museums incline towards the historical and are staffed by people whose academic training and instincts incline them strongly towards narrow specialisation within a given area. While this may be very necessary for the adequate maintenance of historical collections, it militates against an enthusiasm for modern work.[8]

The importance of the Crafts Study Centre's collection is, then, vested in its rarity as one of the very few specific and dedicated craft collections held for that purpose alone in the public domain. Indeed the same is still fundamentally true in 2004, and the Crafts Study Centre is equally rare (perhaps unique in the UK) as a purpose-built museum and gallery for a craft collection. The 'companion' collection, as we have seen, was built up at around the same time in the early 1970s by the Crafts Advisory Committee. The first objects for this national collection were acquired after the British Potters' exhibition held in Germany in 1972. The makers, Leach, Rie, Coper, were all to be featured intensively in the Centre's

collections too, but there seems to have been no strict collaborative
purpose in these two developments.

The Crafts Advisory Committee decisions were driven by exhibition
programming, and the first concept of shaping the collection for
posterity was distinctly unfocused. Victor Margrie comments in the
foreword to the Crafts Council's catalogue of the collection that 'to my
shame, I cannot recall that we had a clear plan as to what to do with [the
objects]; certainly there was no intention to form a permanent
collection'.[9] The ground work for two of the most important public craft

collections in the UK started, then, with a mixture of hope and opportunism, rather than a systematic plan or a determined goal. Both collections, however, were (and still are) largely shaped by makers. The Crafts Study Centre's debt to the practitioners who make up its acquisition committee[10] is immense. They formulated policy, sought out gifts and helped in judicious purchases utilising a budget of merely £2000 a year. The Crafts Council collection also utilised the services of makers, establishing a purchasing committee in 1975 'composed largely of practising craftspeople, with one representative from the museum world… It is hoped that such a committee, coupled with the Council's own close relationship with craftspeople, makes for a constant awareness of developments within the crafts'.[11] This format continues today in the Crafts Council's purchasing panel.

The picture, then, of the development of the crafts in the public domain in the 1970s, was one of fragility: few collections, patchy strategic initiatives, limited opportunities and scarcely any resources. These have never been particular constraints to the growth of cultural organisations in the UK, and the crafts, with singular tenacity and determination, found ways of collaborating and adhering to visionary goals, delivered through these new organisations. The increasing role of the Crafts Council and the funds allocated through the Regional Arts Associations to the crafts gathered momentum from the 1970s onwards. The RAAs steadfastly directed funds to craft makers, and underpinned crucial services such as touring exhibitions, slide indexes, making awards to practitioners, placing craftspeople in school programmes, and nurturing the craft guilds and societies.

Funds from RAAs helped to kick start museum collecting of the contemporary crafts. Eastern Arts, for example, matched funds from the Fitzwilliam Museum's purchase fund to help the purchase of objects, although access to the collections was guarded with some ferocity, as the curator 'must be fairly convinced of the seriousness of the interest before agreeing to make an appointment' to see work not on display.[12] A survey for *Crafts* magazine in 1980 identified 28 museum collections of contemporary craft in England, and of these only the Shipley Art Gallery in Gateshead focused exclusively on crafts. (A less scientific survey for Southern Arts published in *Contemporary Crafts in Museums* in 1996

identified only 22 collections). The Crafts Study Centre has a very special place in 2004 as a dedicated museum of modern crafts, since there has not been dramatic or wholesale change over the past thirty years to this provision. What change there has been, in terms of physical estate, has been driven by the advent of the Lottery.

During 2001 and 2002, a research team brought together for the first time the combined interests and forces of the Heritage Lottery Fund, the Crafts Council and the Arts Council of England. The outcome was a publication *New art for the historic environment*[13] intended to create a wider awareness of the possibilities of using contemporary art and craft to animate the historic environment, from landscapes to parks and heritage settings. The mandatory requirement of Arts Council major lottery schemes to involve artists in capital projects, was a significant driver of new work, and led directly to the creation of what might be described a dispersed national 'collection' of art and craft. Works varied from Peter Freeman's vast lighting scheme for the Lighthouse, Poole, to the most restrained ceremonial lettering at the National Portrait Gallery. Since the start of the lottery (the first grants were awarded in 1995) and up to 2002, the research concluded that some £80 million had been spent on around 350 public art and craft projects, the largest single investment of this type in the UK.

The crafts took only a modest share in this investment. The Arts Council publication *Pride of Place*[14] analysed over 2000 lottery capital projects given grants up to the year 2000, and focused on the physical, as well as social and environmental changes that the works had brought about. Out of these 2000 projects, 55 were focused on the crafts (just under 3% by number) with a total value in grant of £15 million (just under 7% by value), ranging from £6.9 million to the National Glass Centre in Sunderland, to the smallest grant, £2,996 for the Stafford Caribbean Association for refurbishment costs. There are still highly significant capital projects at advanced construction or planning stages, such as the redevelopment of the Devon Guild's headquarters at Bovey Tracey, and the 'Museum of Modern Crafts' at Basingstoke. The fact remains that craft spending from the lottery has been marginal in comparison with other areas. Over the same period, for example, the lottery funded 233 visual arts projects with a grant value of some £170 million.

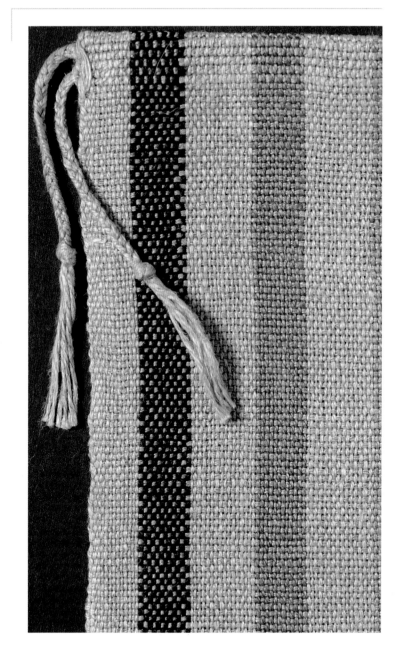

Alison Morton, kitchen towel,
natural linen, 2003

© Alison Morton/
Crafts Study Centre, 2004

One of the features of lottery projects has been the use of craft practitioners to engage creatively in producing work both for heritage refurbishment schemes, and for new buildings. Theatre and Arts Centre projects have been susceptible to this kind of approach. For example, at the Theatre Royal, Winchester, Sue Kennington shaped the overall interior design scheme of a refurbishment project with architects Burrell Foley Fisher. The Quay Arts Centre on the Isle of Wight (a refurbishment project led by Tony Fretton Architects) saw the introduction of a sequence of works for the interior of the building, such as café furniture by Mark Pimlott and a bridge by Jim Partridge. At the Salisbury Arts Centre, a listed church set in a much-loved churchyard, the felling of a yew tree to make way for a new building for the Centre is driving a craft project that will see the seasoned timber reused for craft objects. And at the Crafts Study Centre itself, a regional arts lottery programme award has underpinned the establishment of a team of makers who have worked in a collective environment to produce functional and site specific works for the new building.

The team includes makers at the outset of their professional careers (such as Oliver Russell and Laura Thomas), as well as highly experienced practitioners such as the letter-carver Tom Perkins (who has also designed the new typeface for the title and chapter headings of this book) and the furniture-designer Matthew Burt. Caroline Sharp installed a woven willow piece, as well as creating the landscape design scheme for the front of the new building. Katie Walker made the reception area furniture. The development of the body of work produced by this creative team of practitioners has been led by practical considerations (the need for gallery seating and cases, the requirement for signage or security gates). But the underlying philosophy has been one that emphasises the need to engage craftspeople in all aspects of the Centre's life, from its physical estate to its programme of activity and its research aspirations. The makers have done more than add value to physical fabric; they have proclaimed the message that practitioners are intrinsic to the future of the Crafts Study Centre, as they have been essential to its very derivation and history.

At the start of the 21st century, there has been a cluster of craft museum activity, demonstrating the outcome of (in the main) lottery-funded developments. Major new craft galleries at Manchester Art Gallery and Hove Museum and Art Gallery have been created. The opening of the Hub, at Sleaford in Lincolnshire the 'centre for craft design and making' establishes a significant new and large-scale space for contemporary craft exhibitions. There are refurbished spaces for the crafts at the Shipley Art Gallery, Gateshead, and the 'Show 5' consortium project in 2003 and 2004 presents the work of major craft practitioners in regional galleries as well as at the Crafts Council. *Making it yours* is a significant new series of educational displays drawn from the Crafts Council's collections and shown at Pentonville Road.

The scale of the provision is steadily improving, although it is driven by local initiatives rather than a national plan. The founder Trustees of the Crafts Study Centre would have found these same circumstances in 1970. This may tell us something about the great strength of the craft community (dogged and indefatigable in the face of difficult odds). It also suggests that nationally significant activity can be generated from small organisations, and the remarkable achievements of, for example, The Gallery Ruthin Craft Centre or sates.org,[15] (based at The Winchester Gallery, University of Southampton), are based on sustained curatorship, exhibition planning and publication activity, all delivered by deeply committed staffs invariably small in number.

It may not out of place to record that critical mass for the crafts could be developed with real weight, following on from a concerted and enhanced degree of national planning, as well as an uplift in strategic resources. The collective activity of the crafts infrastructure for the 21st century could be galvanised by even stronger touring networks, more large-scale venues for the presentation of gallery-specific craft shows, and the enhancement of the network of museum collections. A substantial national museum of, and for, the crafts, called for by Christopher Frayling[16] in 2003, might be a bold aspiration for the next phase of post-lottery development. Frayling stated that such a museum would 'exhibit, study and debate the various traditions of the crafts which have emerged over the last century... and locate them within the best of contemporary practice'.

The Crafts Study Centre can fulfil this role (no doubt in partnership with others) from its new headquarters. Although the physical boundaries of the new purpose-built museum and study centre (A & Q Partnership) are not huge, its history and ambitions belie the simple fact of size. The Crafts Study Centre's stature has derived from the vision of its founders, the loyalty of makers who have contributed selflessly to its development, and sustained curatorship, as well as the sterling support of many partner organisations, from funders to museums, arts boards and the Arts and Crafts Councils. A new chapter is about to be written by the Crafts Study Centre and The Surrey Institute of Art & Design, to take the crafts forward in good heart into the twenty-first century.

[1] Unpublished note, Crafts Study Centre archive

[2] Robin Tanner, *Double Harness*, (Impact Books, London, 1987) p179

[3] The Founder Trustees of the Crafts Study Centre were Ewart Uncles (Chairman), Muriel Rose, Robin Tanner, Henry Hammond, Marianne Straub and Christine Smale. The Trustees of the Centre (May 2004) are: Sir Christopher Frayling (Chairman); Pat Carter; Edmund de Waal; Ian Dumelow; Dr Jennifer Harris; Cherry Knott; Duncan Robinson; Peter Sarginson; Heather Smith; Professor Norman Taylor and Amelia Uden.

[4] Crafts Advisory Committee, *Craftsmen of quality* (London, 1976) p6

[5] The deed of gift says 'the object of the charity is the advancement of education of the public in the arts and in particular, artistic crafts in pottery, metal, woven or printed textiles, embroidery or otherwise'.

[6] *20th Century Craftsmanship*, the Holburne of Menstrie Museum, Bath, 10 July-5 August 1972. The exhibition was billed as 'Introducing the Crafts Study Centre Trust'

[7] The membership of the first committee was Richard Dufy (Chairman), Henry Hammond, Heather Child, Peter Sarginson, Marianne Straub and Barley Roscoe

[8] Editorial, *Crafts* 26 (May/June 1977)p.7

[9] Victor Margrie, foreword *Crafts Council collection 1972-1985* (London, 1985) p6

[10] The membership of the committee in 2004 is Christopher Frayling (Chairman), Edmund de Waal, Magdalene Odundo, Takeshi Yasuda, Diana Harrison, Mary Restieaux, John Neilson, Ewan Clayton, Margot Coatts, Lesley Hoskins and Simon Olding

[11] 'Notes on the Collection', *Crafts Council collection 1972-1985* (London, 1985) p9

[12] Quoted in 'Museums Collect', *Crafts* 46 (September/October 1980) p21

[13] Ed., Simon Olding, *New art in the historic environment* (London, 2002)

[14] Ed., Alex Setter, *Pride of place: how the lottery contributed £1 billion to the arts in England* (Arts Council of England, London, 2002)

Credits

Christopher Frayling is Rector of the Royal College of Art, Chairman of the Arts Council England, and has written extensively on the crafts.

Barley Roscoe is a consultant curator, writer and lecturer, and a member of the BBC Antiques Roadshow team of experts. She was responsible for the Crafts Study Centre first within the Holburne Museum of Art, Bath where was Director 1986-1999 and awarded an MBE, and subsequently at the Surrey Institute from 2000-2002.

Edmund de Waal is a potter and writer.

Lesley Millar has been a practising weaver with her own studio since 1975, and has work in the permanent collections of the Crafts Council and Arts Council England, South East. She was awarded a three year Daiwa/AHRB Research Fellowship in contemporary Anglo-Japanese textiles, based at The Surrey Institute of Art & Design in 2001. She has written regularly about textile practice in Britain and Japan, including a monograph on Chiyoko Tanaka.

Ewan Clayton is Visiting Professor in Art, Design, Media and Culture at the University of Sunderland. He teaches Calligraphy at the Roehampton Institute, London, and runs his own lettering business from his home in Brighton. He grew up close to the village of Ditchling in Sussex where he and two earlier generations of his family worked in a Guild of Craftsmen established by Eric Gill.

Matthew Burt (FRSA, FSDC) has been designing and making furniture for thirty years. He remains a passionate advocate for the design led crafts.

Professor Simon Olding was appointed Director of the Crafts Study Centre, The Surrey Institute of Art & Design, University College in 2002. He is Chair of the Ann Sutton Foundation, and a member of the Regional Council of Arts Council England, South West.

Pat Carter has been a Trustee of the Crafts Study Centre for nearly ten years. She is a crafts collector, and has written an introductory book on collecting ceramics.

Photography of the Crafts Study Centre collections and archives.

All of the photographs were taken as part of a major digitisation project at the Crafts Study Centre by David Westwood. The project was funded by the Joint Information Systems Committee (JISC) with additional funds from The Headley Trust, and ran from 2000 to 2004. All of the images (4000 in total) can be seen on the website of the Arts and Humanities Data Service at www.ahds.ac.uk

Every effort has been made to secure the copyright clearance for all of the images used, and where this has been successful, a copyright acknowledgement is made. However, for images on pages 20, 38, 44, 80, 92, 93 and 94 it has not been possible to identify the copyright owner.

The photograph of the Crafts Study Centre on the back cover is by Glen Millington

Acknowledgements

The editors are grateful to the following for their interest in, and support of, the book: the Trustees of the Crafts Study Centre; Tass Mavrogordato; Vivienne Light, Becky Lyle, Jean Vacher and Amanda Fielding. The lettering for the chapter headings and front cover was drawn and designed by Tom Perkins.

The headings were digitized by Fine Fonts (Michael Harvey and Andy Benedek). This lettering is a prototype for a proposed typeface to be released by Fine Fonts.

Essays for the opening of the Crafts Study Centre is published for the Centre's opening to the public in its new home on 1 June 2004 on the Farnham campus of The Surrey Institute of Art & Design, University College.